Break Free From Your Past

ARE YOU DESTINED TO REPEAT PAST MISTAKES? A slave to irrational fears? Do you feel like something is holding you back, blocking your path to happiness and personal fulfillment? Don't let your past—especially your past lives—hold you back!

We all carry attitudes and "lifestyles" from one life to another, repeating past mistakes and reliving fears, until we become aware of these patterns and take positive action to change. *Reincarnation: Remembering Past Lives* shows you how to probe into your own experiences and knowledge—from all of your lives—to understand when and why these patterns started.

With the practical techniques in *Reincarnation: Remembering Past Lives*, learn to enter into your own meditative state to explore the cycles of your lives, release your negative karma, change belief systems that hold you back, build up energy to achieve your goals, connect with your soul mate, and learn many other life-changing practices.

D0067895

About the Authors

Genevieve Lewis Paulson is the director and president of Dimensions of Evolvement, Inc., a non-profit growth center located on 165 acres of the Ozark mountains in Arkansas, a center of psychic, personal, and spiritual learning, accrediting students in the study of Kundalini energy development. In the early 1970s, she founded Sunergos, Inc., a spiritual growth center in Chicago. Where her new experiences might have led her to abandon Western religious beliefs, she instead found a method to meld two varieties of truth, creating a synthesis of two great traditions of belief.

Stephen J. Paulson has been active in the growth field since 1975. He is trained in psychotronics, rebirthing, Swedish massage, Touch for Health, Polarity, Energy Counseling (including reincarnation), and Kundalini. He is Treasurer of Dimensions of Evolvement, Inc., a non-profit growth center. He has five children and three grandchildren. He also operates OEC Publishing which publishes pamphlets and other materials written by Genevieve Lewis Paulson (his mother) and himself.

To Write to the Authors

Both the authors and publisher appreciate hearing from you and learning of your enjoyment of this book and how it has helped you. Llewellyn Worldwide cannot guarantee that every letter written to the authors can be answered, but all will be forwarded. Please write to:

Genevieve Paulson and Stephen J. Paulson
c/o Llewellyn Worldwide
P.O. Box 64383, Dept. K511-8,
St. Paul, MN 55164-0383, U.S.A.

Please enclose a self-addressed, stamped envelope for reply, or $1.00 to cover costs. If outside the U.S.A., enclose international postal reply coupon.

REINCARNATION:
Remembering Past Lives

Genevieve Lewis Paulson &
Stephen J. Paulson

1999
Llewellyn Publications
St. Paul, Minnesota 55164-0383 U.S.A.

FIRST EDITION
Third printing, 1999

Cover design: Lisa Novak
Interior illustrations: Tom Grewe
Editing and book design: Michael Maupin

Library of Congress Cataloging-in-Publication Data

Paulson, Genevieve Lewis, 1927 -
   Reincarnation: remembering past lives / Genevieve Lewis
 Paulson & Stephen J. Paulson. -- 1st ed.
       p.   cm.
   Includes bibliographical references (p. 187) and index.
   ISBN 1-56718-511-8 (trade paper)
   1. Reincarnation. I. Paulson, Stephen J. II. Title
 BL515.P38   1997
 133.9'01'35--dc21   97-20099
                                                        CIP

Llewellyn Worldwide does not participate in, endorse, or have any authority or responsibility concerning private business transactions between our authors and the public.
   All mail addressed to the author is forwarded but the publisher cannot, unless specifically instructed by the author, give out an address or phone number.

Llewellyn Publications
A Division of Llewellyn Worldwide, Ltd.
P.O. Box 64383, Dept. K511-8
St. Paul, MN 55164-0383, U.S.A.
www.llewellyn.com

Printed in the United States of America

Dedication

Genevieve's dedication:
To my children,
Stephen, Kari, Nina, Brad, Roger

Stephen's dedication:
To my wife, *RaeJean*,
and my children,
Wendy, Noel, Brian, Elijah, Hannah
and my grandchildren,
Amber, Alexi, and *Kristen*

Other Publications by Genevieve Lewis Paulson

From Llewellyn Publications:

Meditation and Human Growth (1994)

Kundalini and the Chakras (1991)

From OEC Publishing:

*The Seven Bodies of Man
in the Evolution of Consciousness*

The Seven Eyes in the Evolution of Consciousness

Tests and Steps on the Spiritual Path

For a list of pamphlets and other materials
self-published by Genevieve Lewis Paulson and
Stephen J. Paulson, please contact:

*OEC Publishing
HC 77, Box 777
Melbourne, AR 72556*

Acknowledgments

Special thanks to Ralph Thiel, who not only put the entire manuscript on computer, through many revisions, but helped with editing as well. A special thanks for his patience and steadfastness.

Thanks to Anne Thiel, Nancy Steinbeck, and Alice Shewmaker for proofreading and comments, and to Diana Korte for all her help.

Many thanks, also, to workshop participants, as well as those who have had private sessions, for exploring these areas with us.

Table of Contents

XIV Future   175

Bibliography   185

Index   187

List of Meditations

Preface

THE PROCESS OF REINCARNATION PRESENTS a wonderful way of expanding one's knowledge so that a greater perspective of who we are and what our potentials are may be realized. Persons will find they have experienced many different ways of being, been involved in many areas of career or in expressing their talents, as well as having lived in various areas of the world.

Throughout these many lives, people will have had the opportunity to experience many religious traditions that have served to fill a need to worship something higher than themselves, in the hopes of discovering a greater way of being. Different concepts and different terminologies have developed. These authors were raised in the Christian tradition and, therefore, use the word "God" for the ultimate power. We hope readers will insert the word or words of their choice when they see the word "God."

Introduction
VALUES OF PAST LIFE KNOWLEDGE

Is KNOWLEDGE OF PAST LIVES of any real value to a person's present life? Shouldn't the past remain buried? There are those who think not. Similar to our childhoods, our past lives contain events that may have caused us to see things in an emotional or irrational way, or there may have been very traumatic events that have caused blocks to future growth and joys. Many times trauma, limited perception, or deep emotional involvement in an event that we were unable to see clearly or as well as we'd like may affect not only the remainder of that particular life, but in many lives to follow. Attitudes can be formed that hold us back from healthy growth, enjoyment of life, or satisfying relationships with others. Taking a look into past lives is much the same as going into a person's childhood in analysis to weed out the fears and misunderstandings planted there, as well as to heal emotional or mental wounds.

Irrational fears in a present life, such as fear of fire or animals, with no known cause, can sometimes be traced back to events in previous lives. These events, when understood or even looked at again, can sometimes bring immediate release from the fear or problem, or bring a beginning of a release. An example of immediate release is in the case of a young woman who used to lie awake at night and think of stabbing people in the back. She wondered why she felt that way; she had no known reason for the urge and it troubled her a good deal. She was not a violent person in this life, but a past life reading showed a recent life as a man with mental illness who had stabbed several persons. Since the awareness of this she says she has had no return of the feelings and she has become much more at peace with herself.

In regressions another factor becomes very evident. People have strong tendencies to carry their attitudes and "lifestyle" from one life to another, until such time as they gain awareness of how they are behaving and an awareness that this is not the way they wish to live. When a person can face the fact that she alone is responsible for her actions, as well as reactions, thoughts, and attitudes, then it becomes easier to make a change. Although a change in one's life ultimately depends on oneself, others can help or hinder that change. Also, events can and do happen, which a person has no control over. It is possible, however, to have control over one's own feelings and reactions to the event and what it does to the personality.

What of the person who says, "I just couldn't help myself!" and seemingly could not? This may be true at the time, but the person is the product of his earlier life and previous lives and the way he reacts is usually pre-determined by earlier choices. If a person wishes to change and make different choices—and does—behavior becomes different as well.

For example, a woman in her thirties has trouble in this life trusting people or accepting them with their imperfections. In a regression it was found she had lived several lives the same way. Her dreams, as a young woman, were of having a home, husband and family. They were beautiful but were never fulfilled. She could not trust enough to love. She indicated she still felt the same way in this life. The knowledge that she was repeating a non-productive pattern can help free her to make changes.

In another example, a man who was regressed back several lives ago re-experienced a time when he saw a woman crushed by a falling building. He felt incapable of helping her, and hurriedly left the scene when he became fearful of the woman's dog, which stayed beside her. He experienced guilt feelings over her death and thought he would be blamed for not saving her and hid in a forest for many years, living the life of a hermit. He stayed in the forest until his death—never forgetting that he did not try to help. This event explained to him why he would tell himself quite often in this lifetime, "If I ever see anyone in trouble, I won't run away from them. I'll try to help." He is, in this lifetime, very willing to help. He needed to go back into that experience, not only for understanding, but also to forgive himself. The need to forgive ourselves is as great as the need to forgive others. Awareness of that past life can also help him be more clear in whether or not he should help someone.

People don't always run away to escape from unbearable situations. Sometimes they just give up and die, or commit suicide. The need to escape unbearable situations or just plain boring existences, unhappy home lives or unsuccessful careers occurs more often than most of us know. The situations are there, however, for a reason. If there is something there to experience and learn from and we run away from it, a similar situation or opportunity to learn and grow will reappear. We cannot forever run away from our learning experiences. If we do not face them in one life, they will appear in another life where they are usually stronger because of the force from before. Getting in touch with happy or satisfying lives has been rewarding to some. One woman whose life has been filled with much trouble and unhappiness will, when she is depressed, relax for a few minutes and remember a former life when her dying thoughts were happy ones because she felt she had done everything she was supposed to do and everything worked out well. This gives her renewed courage and strength to go ahead in this life.

Another value in re-experiencing portions of past lives is in the realization that you are you, regardless of whatever race, shape, size or sex you may be. Some bodies are better looking, some are easier to live in, but you are still you, regardless of the physical body that houses you.

To fully realize the autonomy of one's self can be a very freeing or a very frightening experience, or both. The courage to take full responsibility for one's self is just not there all at once. It has to be acquired one step at a time. It takes courage to look at one's self, to look objectively and question, "Is this the way I want to be, the way I want to live?" Then more courage is needed to make the change and to stick with it! (The phrase, "Courage is letting go of the predictable or usual" seems to apply here.)

We believe that most people are not afraid of change. In fact, many long for it. What they fear is not understanding the "why and how" of the change. If they had a user's manual for their lives it would help. Actually, the astrological chart is the closest thing we have to a personal user's manual.

Past life knowledge can help us find causes of problems that many times will bring insights for better solutions. Past life knowledge can give the calmness that comes from realizing there is a plan for our lives and development. It can bring an acceptance of death as another part of life. Most important, however, is to remember that each life is a new opportunity for growth and development and in each life, each day is a new beginning.

Another very important aspect of opening to past lives is to regain some of the skills and abilities that were available for us to use in former lives. We never lose any knowledge or abilities; however, we do lose the use of them for a variety of reasons, including being in a different environment where particular skills are not taught or held in high esteem (such as healing forms), being in a different astrological pattern for the purpose of learning some new skills, or not remembering that such skills were possible. Sometimes it is possible to relive spiritual experiences that happened in previous lives or to re-experience joy, great love or other more expansive emotions and attitudes than a person currently enjoys.

Chapter 1
PAST LIFE EXAMPLES

REINCARNATION IS AN INCREDIBLY complex process. Each person's experiences can be vastly different, yet somehow, the same. In the following examples, gathered from clients, you may find information that resonates with you or opens your consciousness to some of your own experiences. You will note the clients were at home being either male or female. The gender is important sometimes because it puts a person in a position where the lessons can be learned easier.

Example 1: The Winner

This man had been an Arabian horse trader. He was "out to win" and really enjoyed bargaining. Meeting others and bargaining was a game for him. In this life he still enjoys meeting people and still strives to win; however, he now looks for opportunities to help others "win" as well.

In another life he was known as an excellent dancer, part of the Watusi tribe. He was learning grace and control of the body. However, he died young in a tribal skirmish. That gave him some fear of vulnerability of the physical body. In his current life he is too preoccupied with body and health.

This person has done well with the "win-win" attitude he's adopted; however, his preoccupation with his health has actually caused greater problems.

Example 2: Finding Balance

This lady went back to a life where she saw art as a waste of time and thought that it had no value. Then one day she understood the expression in it and realized the value of creativity for its own sake, not necessarily having value only in the finished product.

She then spent a number of lifetimes excessively experiencing different ways of creating—pottery, painting, as well as other forms.

Another life she was an excessively firm schoolteacher.

Her tendencies through her lives were to be "all this" or "all that." Now, she is trying to keep a balance.

Example 3: The Aloof Ruler

This person had a ruling role. She was very aloof, so she didn't know the struggles that the common people endured. This life she still uses aloofness as well as other means to avoid relating.

Another life she was a Chinese lady and enjoyed the "role." It was a pleasant life, but after death she had a sense of "what for" or "what was the life about?"

The next life she was a man who studied and practiced healing with herbs and potions and helped many people.

The first two lives brought this person to the third life where she/he learned to work with others in meaningful ways. This current life is a continuation of working with and helping others.

Example 4: The Pleasure Princess

This woman had been a princess in Egypt and enjoyed the life and would have liked that life this time. She had all the lovers she wanted and gorgeous jewelry. It was a life of pleasure. She didn't understand the misery of the people.

There was a tendency in the past to understand only where the self was. In the current life she is learning to understand others and to share her good fortune. She still likes pleasure, lovers, and beautiful jewelry.

Example 5: A Search for Macho Energy

This person had died in the Crimean War. As he died, he wondered about the futility of war. He had just broken up with a beautiful girl, so he didn't mind dying.

As a woman in an African life, she was in love with a macho, older married man, but married a man her age who was rather timid. This life she does not want a relationship with a timid man. She is still looking for macho energy.

Later, in a life in Korea, he was a male student of ancient scriptures; however, he wouldn't share any of his knowledge. In this life the pendulum has swung and the person (again female) wants to share knowledge and is also developing her own feminine "macho."

Example 6: The Student of Life

This person had a number of lives immersed in study, especially law. She didn't spend much time experiencing life, preferring, instead, to retreat into books. She then went through several lives where learning was kept from her so that she would develop relationships.

This life she is balancing learning from books and from relationships. She learned that if she wanted to pass a test she needed to spend some time with friends beforehand.

Example 7: Understanding God's Will

This person had a number of lives in which she was trying to understand the relationship of pleasure, duty, and religion. She was told too many times that sex and other pleasures were not God's will.

One life she was a mother of six highly unusual children, brilliant and in leadership positions. She wondered, "Where did they come from?" They didn't seem like hers and she felt inferior to them.

Another life she lived a very frugal life, worked hard and gave most of what she had to others.

This life she is working on self-esteem, balance, and developing her own philosophy of life.

Example 8: A Dancer for Love

This person had been an exotic dancer with very intricate movements. She came to the attention of a ruler, who became enamored with her. He turned away from his wife, family, and then country, resulting in almost total destruction of all he had.

This life she is afraid of anyone loving her "too much." She is also afraid of loving others deeply as well. She needs to balance love with common sense.

Example 9: The Reformed Rake

This person had a number of lives where the pursuit of women was his downfall. He was quite a swashbuckler in France when that was in style! He liked and still likes intrigue, uncovering deceits, and is at his best in impossible situations.

This life he is learning a gentler way of being and he is learning to use his energies creatively as well as through problem solving.

Example 10: The Horse Trainer

This person had a strong life of training horses and was excellent in this field. This life he would rather train people. However, they don't want to be trained in the manner he wants to train them.

He had envied rulers in some lives, later became a ruler, and then realized the unsettled and difficult role they have. He realized ruling others wasn't that great or easy.

This life he needs to develop a more realistic and usable leadership style.

Example 11: The Healer

This person had a number of lives devoted to the healing arts. In this life he is studying and becoming aware of many forms of healing. He is devoted to this field during his current life and to bringing a synthesis to his medical work.

He had a life as an English gentleman and learned the importance of life and respect for it. He still carries the bearing and attitudes of that life today, which gives him greater effectiveness in his work.

Chapter II
PROCESS OF REINCARNATION

WHY DO WE REINCARNATE ANYWAY? Why do we go through this process? Some say God, or whatever you call the supreme energy, has created us for companionship, others say God grows and develops as we grow and develop. Whatever the reason, there is a force in the universe called life of which we are all PARTAKERS—which pulls us on this path of growth. As a plant reaches towards the light, so do we reach towards enlightenment. In this reach towards enlightenment we start as unconscious sparks of God-consciousness and reincarnate over and over so that we become fully conscious parts of God-consciousness. We become individuated, but also a part of the whole and co-creators with God in the Divine plan. The greater truth behind this process may only be apparent when we have completed it.

How Does It Work?

The process of growth through reincarnation goes slowly, much more than most people imagine. It is possible to have many thousands of lives on this earth, some short and others much longer. Much depends on how quickly the person grows and how interested she is in the process. It is possible to accomplish the growth of many lifetimes in one life. Other persons grow so slowly that, although they may be considered "old souls" or as having had more lives than normal, they may just be slow growers. For the most part when a person is called an "old soul" it is usually meant that she is a "wise soul."

When a person re-experiences past lives, one of the most notable aspects is that she will feel very similar to how she is today. The essence or soul energy of the person permeates all of her lives. Since the body shape, size, and color may be very different and life circumstances may be totally different, it is important to realize that we are much greater than our bodies or personalities. Sensing the soul essence or "I amness" in past lives helps to recognize it in this life.

The soul never dies; it is the eternal part of us. The soul invests in the personality and body so it can develop itself further.

Although people are very aware of the life in the body, sometimes they are not as aware of the personality's function on the astral, mental, and other higher planes. Meditation helps develop not only the awareness of life on these planes, but also helps to develop it.

Karma and Growth

Our main purpose in life is our development. However, in our paths we sometimes create imbalances, are not fair to others or ourselves, and thus we create what is sometimes called karma. In eastern terminology karma means "to balance." In Christian terms it is explained as "A man reaps what he sows," (Gal. 6:7, *The New English Bible*).

Some people think that we live over and over again in order to complete or balance karma. If the sole purpose of reincarnation was to balance karma, why start? In our work we've seen over and over the person's pull towards enlightenment, to development. When people really work toward this goal, there is a sense of purpose and a joy in living, and karma is not so readily developed.

People caught in the "wheels" of karma are more liable to be negative and feel purposeless. Each time we learn new things it helps us understand life and balance, and less karma is created. It is important, then, that we have greatly varied lives in order to develop more fully.

We will have had lives as poor persons, rich persons, successful by worldly standards or very unsuccessful, lonely lives, lives filled with love and companionship. We will experience all ways of being, as well as all races.

Occasionally a person will change sex for a life or several lives in order to gain understanding or work out karma (balance) that could best be done by changing gender. This change of gender happens so that new opportunities can be experienced in the gender for which they can only happen. (See Chapter IV for further information on karma.)

Family Groups

In this evolutionary plan we start out in our journey as part of a "family group," which may include many hundreds or even thousands of souls. There are also "tribes" of these families that incarnate together and work toward all reaching the fulfillment of their journey together. Some persons come from other planets to aid in this process and may be assigned to reincarnate over and over to teach or lead the particular group to which they are assigned.

Almost all of one's reincarnating is done with your "family." That means you have seen your mothers, fathers, brothers, sisters, children, best friends, lovers and co-workers over and over again. You learn to relate to persons in many roles and many ways until you finally reach a "universal friendship" level with them. There is no such thing as completing karma with someone and then being done with them. It is more of completing karma and then developing the universal friendship.

As we go through these lives over and over, it is much like children playing house. "You were the mother yesterday, I want to be the mother today. Okay, then, I'll be Uncle Harry." Last life you were the mother, this life the child. Sometimes children will have such a strong subliminal memory of being the parent that they want to "parent the parent" and direct their own lives as they see fit.

If we have set a particularly difficult task for ourselves in a coming life, we may look for a situation where we will be with someone who has been a source of strength and comfort before. Or it may be the person wishes to help because you helped him or her previously. Also, there may be a particular group who has given strength and love to each other in different capacities many times before. If this continues too much they may find that the "wheel of karma" holds them apart so they begin to develop other relationships as well.

Wheels of Karma

There are many ways to look at the concept of the wheel of karma. There can be a "wheel" between persons—where "A" does "B" in and during a later life "B" does "A" in. They continue their relationship connected with this wheel of energy (see Figure 1, page 12), which pulls them back again and again to deal with one another, until such time as one of the persons recognizes what is going on and chooses to take away his or her energy from the wheel effect and turn it to other uses. Sometimes this wheel happens in love relationships that have not been honest or truly loving to one another. It can also happen in business or political relationships. When one person realizes what is going on and makes the necessary changes, he is then released from this wheel. The other person, however, rolls his wheel around until he can connect it with someone else in a similar situation, or until he begins to learn and change.

We can also create our own wheels of behavior where we go round and round with the same way of being and reacting to life. It is surprising how often a person's character stays the same for a number of lives. Patterns are repeated until the person has some sort of awakening experience that takes him or her beyond their present awareness. This allows a bigger vision of life, recognizing new possibilities and allowing new ways of being to emerge.

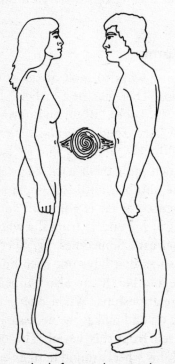

Figure 1. There is a wheel of energy between these two people from the navel chakra, which indicates they have emotional issues to release. Either person may pull away by understanding the situation and redirecting the energy.

—Meditation—
Wheels of Karma

Be in a meditative state.
    a. With whom do you feel you have a wheel
       of karma going?

    b. Can you let go of it?

    c. Do you have your own wheel of behavior
       to contend with?

    d. Can you let go of it?

Especially during this period of more rapid growth in our evolution it is a good time to put yourself into situations where you can learn new ways of being or comprehend greater visions or have the possibility of wider experiences. This helps to stop character repetition. For example, if you are a very intellectual person, you may have been into that for many, many lives until you have overbalanced yourself. Then you may be in a life where that is denied to you. An example is a man who was crazy about music and couldn't even learn to play the simplest instrument. Nothing would work for him. He had spent so many lives in music that it was denied him during this particular life. Now he has to learn to create harmony in other aspects of life, especially relationships.

Another example is when a person has been quite egotistical and self-centered in one life and totally against others who are different. In another life that person may be of the same race or group that he or she previously hated. Sometimes, instead of trying to understand the energy of the race or group, the person may still be as egotistical and self-centered in the newer life and hate someone else. It will then require more experiences for the person to learn understanding and love.

—Meditation—
Free Will

Be in a meditative state.
> *a. Is my free will encumbered by emotional or mental attachments that hold me back?*

> *b. How have I used my free will to further my development?*

Created Equal

Different tribes may begin their paths at different times from other tribes. This makes some souls "older" than others. We start out with our "tribes" and go back with them as well.

When a particular tribe or group of families starts out, all members are equal to one another. What a person does with his consciousness can be very different after that. We have free will to make the kind of growth we wish.

Some people enjoy growing and developing and will use more of their free will in these areas. Others may use their free will to just get by. Some people will make great strides in some lives and make very little growth other times. Much of this depends on what a person believes. If the belief system is rigid there will be narrow vision and the feeling of "stuckness" can result. Persons who are rigid often become more rigid until something happens to shake them out of their narrow space.

Another way of looking at free will is to see if one's own will is free of heavy emotional or mental attachments or free of karma from the past. By this we mean that a person may be so caught in emotions, attitudes, or prejudices that those energies have the stronger force. In this case, a person may want to do something, yet can't seem to get it together.

Also, karma set in motion previously may be stronger than the person's will and that will have to be balanced before the free will of the current time can be set in motion.

Cycles of Lives

In our work with regressions it has been very obvious that people have a series of lives in order to explore all aspects of a particular quality. For instance, a person may be working on power. She may spend several lives being powerless, some lives being the power behind the throne, some in power, some in misuse of power against others or against herself, some powerless until she understands all aspects of power, including physical, emotional, mental and spiritual levels.

If a person were in a cycle of healing, the line would include experiencing illness, treated or untreated, healing others, studying causes of illness, or developing healthier bodies. These lives will not necessarily be in chronological order.

—Meditation—
Cycles

Be in a meditative state.
  a. What seems to be the main learning in this life?

  b. Does it seem to be part of a cycle?

Sometimes people will feel that they are in a last life or may be told that they are in a last life. Usually they are in the last life of a cycle. People attached to the idea that the current life is the last may find that they return again in order to lose that attachment and to appreciate the process of life and growth. Advanced persons who do not need to reincarnate don't really mind if they do or do not. Wherever they can serve God and the Divine plan best is what matters to them.

Reincarnating on Lower Levels

Sometimes there is a tendency to judge others about where they are in their growth. This is very difficult to do as a person may be highly advanced and come back in a lowly life to be with others in that station of life in order to help or comfort them. Or it may be that the person becomes a focal point for other growth by appearing to be lesser developed. We shouldn't judge others because it pulls us into their pattern of existence in order to understand it. We do need to discern what is right or wrong for us, though, as we are responsible for where we are and what we do. We don't know the overall patterns of others.

Some people feel that they have lived more developed lives previously or are told by psychics that they are "fallen masters." This usually refers to someone who has achieved great growth in many areas, but did not use it correctly and has to repeat some lessons.

Many people are afraid they might reincarnate on lower levels if they have not lived "right." If lessons are better learned from a lower level of life, then that may happen. However, the total growth is so important that such a life can be worth it. The good things already learned are not lost, but are waiting until the person is ready to access those attributes again.

In our work with regressions we've seen a number of times when a person has achieved great abilities, but disdained his or her human life and left that underdeveloped. These persons then returned to a life filled with human experience. We must fully develop in all areas in order to complete these earthly sojourns.

The Holographic Cosmos

Michael Talbot, in his book *The Holographic Universe*, explores the cosmos as a hologram. He refers to some of Karl Pibram's ideas: "Was it possible, (Pibram) wondered, that what the mystics had been saying for centuries was true, reality was maya, an illusion, and what was out there was really a vast resonating symphony of wave forms, a 'frequency domain' that was transformed into the world as we know it only after it entered our senses?" We believe that through our bodies, mind, spirit, and senses we have almost magical abilities to create our own realities. It's as though we can pull from the holographic cosmos or "soup" whatever we need or want in our lives. It seems that there are many realities possible and that the greatest illusion is to think that only one is correct. All realities have their own validity, but not a total validity.

People who deeply experience other dimensions in the dream state, through meditative states, or by sudden insights or peak experiences, recognize a completely different reality from the usual human one. The more we can open to other realities the easier our human one will be, because we have a greater awareness of possibilities.

Through this holographic "soup," which contains everything—past, present, future, manifested and unmanifested energies and concepts—we draw, through resonance of vibrations, greater understanding and new ways of being. In this holographic universe or "soup" is a primordial substance called akasha upon which is imprinted not only each person's personal record, but also everyone else's. When a person develops the ability to go into these energies, they can not only read their own akashic records, but also read others' information. We can learn from the experiences recorded on the akasha (see Chapter VI).

Also, we all tap into what is called the collective unconscious. This energy contains the total of the human experience, with its fears and depravity but also its learning and growth. As we develop new skills in the human area, the essence of that development goes into the collective unconscious. As we turn negative tendencies into positive ones, that also affects the collective unconscious. We can and do draw from this energy pool of experience to help in our lives.

There is also a universal stream of consciousness, which contains the spiritual achievements of people. That is also available for us to draw from. All of these energies are a part of the holographic cosmos.

Lives Out of Order

Because of the holographic cosmos and the omnipresence of time, we do not have to live our lives in chronological order. We may have already completed some life that normally would be considered as best lived at some future time. Or we may yet have to live some incarnations that we would consider best lived in the past.

The concept of a holographic universe helps explain this. In the holographic universe, with no boundaries for time and space, past, present, and future all seem suspended in the holographic soup.

If we get deeply into some growth or study, we may pull, through some resonance of similar vibrations, a future life that would not normally be available until its scheduled later time.

When this happens, a person usually feels that she can't quite learn or fulfill all desires. It's as though she is short of some experiences or knowledge that would make this life easier and more profitable in growth and accomplishment. It doesn't mean that the person won't achieve much, it just means she has to work harder. It's as though a fourth grader were suddenly thrust into the ninth grade.

If a person lives a life that was normally scheduled in the past and was skipped, the person may feel bored and held back. He may feel left out and that there is much more to his abilities than he can readily tap into. It's as though in this case the ninth grader is thrust into the fourth grade.

Working with Kundalini, the evolutionary force, or developing spiritual awareness and concentration usually helps a person to expand beyond limitations that may arise from either past or future lives out of order.

In this book we hope to explore many aspects of reincarnation to help people achieve greater fulfillment of their current life.

Why Don't We Remember?

One of the most commonly heard questions regarding reincarnation is, "If this is true why don't I remember any of my past lives?" The answer has several parts. How much of your childhood do you remember? What about those fleeting memories of having been someplace you know you haven't been in this life? Or of "knowing" someone you have just met? What about knowing how to do something you have never been shown or taught in this life? What about dreams of other times, other places, other situations? Not all of these are symbolic. Do you spend any time in meditation and the development of the part of your mind that houses these memories? What if you honestly cannot remember anything even remotely connected with a past life, yet you are intensely interested and want to know? Chapter VI may give you some help in accessing your past.

Chapter III
PROCESS OF EVOLUTION

REINCARNATION IS NOT AS SIMPLE as just being born over and over again, trying to make up for past mistakes. It is part of a much more complex process— evolution. To approach reincarnation without the greater picture of evolution distorts the picture. It is similar to taking one particular year as being the only important part of life.

Reincarnation is part of the process of the evolution of consciousness. It is being born into bodies time after time, for the purpose of developing consciousness, and becoming fully enlightened beings. Some of these lives deal, however, more with balancing things that previously happened (karma) rather than making great strides in development.

Between our earth (or other planet) lives there is also great growth in comprehension and expansion of possibilities. We review what we have done, plan for future lives and study with our spiritual guides. The life between lives has much activity in it. Although some people may rest for great periods of time due to stresses incurred in Earth life, most people are busy getting a clearer picture of their evolution.

Some people say life on Earth isn't real. It is only a dream episode from the greater life on the other side. This is true in many ways, however, the sojourn into the bodies on Earth has its own reality and its own importance. Living in a body on Earth (or another planet) allows you to take action, to change energies, to create. Also, God works through our bodies to help in various ways.

Importance of Earth

Each of the planets in our solar system has specific energies. For example, Mars has the vibration of mental and war-like attitudes, while Venus has the vibrations of beauty, art, and love. Our Earth is blessed with energies for growth. Its main purpose is to grow things and this includes humans as well. The particular Earth energy that speeds human growth and evolution is called Kundalini (Sanskrit for "circular power"). This energy causes people to evolve at a much faster rate than they might on other planets. This makes Earth a valuable place to embark on more intense growth.

One of the nice things we can do with Earth is to help it grow plants and animals as well as humans. We then are helping Earth fulfill its purpose.

Big Bang Theory

In *A Brief History of Time,* Stephen Hawking writes: "...In 1929, Edwin Hubble made the landmark observation that wherever you look, distant galaxies are moving rapidly away from us. In other words, the universe is expanding...Hubble's observation suggested that there was a time, called the Big Bang, when the universe was infinitely small and infinitely dense."

After the Big Bang, the universe began the process of expansion. Since we are a part of this universe, there is a natural movement also of our consciousness to expand. It's as though the expanding movement of our universe pulls our consciousness with it. It's as though each of us is a "Big Bang" and that we continue to have "Big Bangs" when our consciousness or evolution takes a leap.

Everything has that sense of expansion or opening. If people try to hold it back, it creates irritability, then restlessness, and then explosiveness.

Awareness—when not interfered with—has a natural tendency to expand. When a person has a peak experience it speeds the consciousness expansion process, also.

Expanding Consciousness

As we continue our search for meaning and understanding of our processes, we need to expand our comprehension to greater possibilities and more expansive concepts. Many people get caught up in what is the right belief system. This can actually hold a person back as it makes a rather rigid mindset and it becomes difficult to open to more comprehensive views. As we grow we can conceive more, and new things become possible for the individual. Then, as further evolution or expansion happens, we can conceive of even greater possibilities.

Evolution: Personal and Genetic

Evolution is of two main parts. One is personal, the evolution of consciousness of the individual. The other is genetic and brings the evolution of the physical body. Compare our abilities with those we know of cave people and you will find we have made great strides in our potentials. The decade of the '90s is one that has such strong evolutionary energies that we will make a major quantum leap in our evolution of our consciousness. So much growth will be made that a few decades ago will seem rather primitive to us also.

—Meditation—
Evolution of the Body and the Person

Since space is expanding and things are moving further apart, we find changes with us as well. Things happen on the personal level much as on the cosmic level.

Be in a meditative state.

> *a. Feel your body's energy expanding. Feel the expansion of your body's consciousness.*
>
> *b. Ask which is more expansive, your body's consciousness or yours?*
>
> *c. If your body is more expansive, ask your personal consciousness to expand to match it.*

d. What could you accomplish if the personal matched the body consciousness?

e. Ask to know three things holding back your personal consciousness.

f. If your personal consciousness is more expanded than your body's, then ask your body to expand its consciousness to match your consciousness, at least momentarily.

g. What could you accomplish if your body's consciousness matched your consciousness?

h. Ask to know three things that are holding back the evolution of your body. Is part of the problem genetic? Maybe you've inherited a denser body? If so, is there a reason you came into a denser body? Your body is the result of generations of development; some are lighter and refined, however.

i. Meditate on the two tracks: you (reincarnation) and your body (generation after generation). Let your body float. Free up your body. Let your consciousness be free and open. Can you sense a greater potential?

Evolution of Species/Consciousness

In the evolution of the species approach, some people believe the Darwinian theory which states we develop from lesser animal forms than ourselves. The physical connecting links, however, remain elusive. It may be that the links are on consciousness levels instead of, or as well as, physical levels.

In the evolution of consciousness approach, we begin as pure energy, however, an underdeveloped form of energy. We need to travel through different life forms (see Figure 2 below) to develop and expand our intelligence, abilities, and awareness. When we have learned all we can from one form (minerals, plants, and animals) we make a jump in consciousness to the next highest form.

The following meditation can give you the opportunity to experience this possibility. Let your mind be open to this experience and see if it brings you any new understanding or information that may be useful to you.

You may wish to put this meditation on tape to facilitate the experience or have someone lead you on it. Give yourself plenty of time to experience the different energies. Some people prefer to listen to background music.

When you have finished the meditation you may wish to make notes of your experience. Doing this sometimes brings more information.

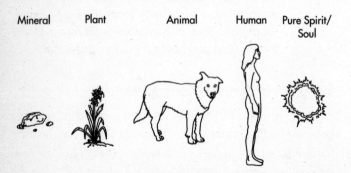

Mineral   Plant   Animal   Human   Pure Spirit/
Soul

Figure 2. Forms for Evolution of Species/Consciousness

—Meditation—
Journey through Time

This journey through time can open you up to your experiences. Lie down. Be in a comfortable position.

Begin peaceful deep breathing. Breathe all the way to the ends of your toes, the ends of your fingers, and the top of your head. Feel your energy expanding as you do this. Let your consciousness expand. Be open to what comes. Don't judge, analyze, doubt, or pick apart. You can do that when the exercise is over. Take this time now to just experience.

Continue to feel relaxed but now add a sense of heaviness. Let yourself feel very, very heavy. Sink into the floor. Then let the heaviness go and let yourself be filled with lightness. Let yourself float. Now be heavy and float at the same time. This is a way of getting yourself into the state of dual awareness we are reaching for in this meditation, an awareness of who you are today, who you have been, and who you will be. Continue to feel the heavy and light at the same time but don't over-concentrate on it.

We start our journey as undeveloped sparks of God-consciousness. We go through countless lives, countless experiences, some on this planet, some on others, in order to become totally conscious parts of God-consciousness. Not only co-creators in our evolution, our own personal evolution, but also co-creators in the destiny of our universe. Our journeys are a part of the divine plan toward enlightenment. As a plant reaches towards the sun, so we reach towards enlightenment.

We start our descent into matter from pure energy. Feel yourself as that pure energy, that undeveloped spark of God-consciousness waiting to evolve, learn, and grow.

Feel the descent into matter by going into the mineral world. *Imagine that you are a grain of sand on the beach. You have no will of your own, no movement of your own. The water washes you back and forth, the wind blows you. There is heat, there is cold. You feel them but there is no developed sense of warmth or cold in terms of feeling good or not good, only an awareness, a sensation. As a grain of sand on the beach there is nothing to worry about, nothing to think about. You are not able to make even a sound by yourself. In this part of evolution you develop an awareness in the physical sense.*

Then ages and ages pass and you are now ready for a step up in evolution and you find you are ready to be part of the plant kingdom. *Imagine that you are a plant. You still have your physical awareness that you developed as a mineral, but you now have the beginning of an emotional awareness, the beginning of feelings. What feelings do you experience as the plant? Also in this step in evolution, movement has been added. Roots that go into the Earth and the top part of yourself that reaches to the sun. Feel the beginnings of movement. Can you make a sound as your leaves rub together?*

Ages pass and you are now ready for another step in evolution, this time into the animal kingdom. *Through your time in the mineral and plant kingdoms you will have developed and increased physical abilities and sensations. You will also have developed some emotional abilities. You find that in this step of evolution you are now starting to develop mental abilities, beginning to think and to remember. Think of an animal for which you have an affinity. Be that animal. Feel it, experience it. What's it like to have the animal's expanded physical, emotional, and mental abilities? What is life like for you now? Mobility, too, is increased. You are not tied to roots going into the ground. You can move around. You can walk, you can run, you can stop in various places. Experience the movement, the freedom of movement. What does it feel like? What kinds of sounds can you make to express yourself?*

More and more ages pass and you are now ready for another step in evolution, that of entering the human kingdom. *This level has the beginning of spirit. We are made in the image of God. Spiritual things are available to us since we have a spirit. Also, we have much greater developed physical, emotional, and mental abilities. The mobility has increased. Walking, running, climbing, swimming, riding animals, building and using boats. Eventually as humans we will build cars, trains, airplanes.*

Be a cave person. Feel the beginning of spiritual awareness. How does that manifest for you? Feel your increased physical, emotional, and mental abilities. Feel your new development. How do you experience your increased mobility? How has your ability to express yourself through sound increased?

Time passes. Be in a life in the period between A.D. *1400 and 1700. How have your physical abilities increased? How have your emotions developed? What new mental abilities do you have? How has your spiritual awareness developed? What kind of mobility do you have? How has your ability to express yourself through sound increased? Do you include music in your sounds?*

Time passes and we come to the period of now. Be yourself as you are now. *Really be and experience your current self. Feel the increased awareness in the physical level. What physical abilities do you now have? How have you developed emotionally? Mentally? Spiritually? How has your mobility increased? How has your ability to express yourself through sound increased?*

Time passes and we go through a quantum leap in evolution and you become a super person. Feel your stronger, healthier body. Feel the emotions, how refined and expressive they are because of expanded mental abilities and spiritual development. Be aware also of your expanded consciousness, your expanded awareness that can know many, many things that were not known to you before. Things that were beyond your seeing, or beyond your hearing are now available to you. What is life like now? How do you express yourself through sound now?

Then go ahead in time until you are fully developed as an entity. You do not have to reincarnate if you do not wish to. You are not bound by time or space. You are fully enlightened and a co-creator with the God-force. You may be called god-like. How does that feel? Your mobility has increased to the point where you can think of where you want to be and be there. Your ability to express yourself with sound has progressed to the point to where you can send thoughts any place you wish, just with energy. You do not need a body to form the sounds. What does this feel like to be fully developed? And now you are back home. Back home with the God-force from which you left eons ago as an unconscious spark of God-consciousness. You have returned as a fully conscious, fully aware spark of the God-consciousness. Meditate on that thought for a few more moments. Bring as much of that enlightened energy as you can back to the present day.

Stretch well and be aware of thoughts and feelings for a few minutes.

Chapter IV
KARMA

KARMA IS A SANSKRIT WORD that means "to balance." It can also be explained as reaction follows action, or you get back what you send out. It deals with the principle of cause and effect. If you do wrong to someone, that energy will have to be balanced. It may mean that the person will do a similar wrong to you at some other time or it may mean that you will sometime understand the consequences of your actions and decide to change your attitude and behavior. When you gain understanding of your thought or action it releases some of the karmic force. Usually by taking corrective action yourself you will change the energy enough so you are no longer under the karmic retribution.

For instance, if you have been negative or deceitful and recognize it and make changes, it is possible that you may undo any wrong done. You will have balanced it right away.

Although karma means to balance, it is more generally thought of as paying for bad deeds. Sometimes people will also create good karma, which means that they will have done good deeds that will sometimes bring back good to them.

Good karma may be misunderstood. However, it seems that doing good deeds for the purpose of receiving good karma is great. However, if a person becomes attached to this, they may find the good karma coming at inopportune times and in strange ways.

Bad karma may be thought of as lack of growth and understanding that only the hard knocks of unpleasant experience can develop. For example, cruel treatment of others might require experiencing a later time of receiving cruel treatment. This would then bring consideration and compassion for others. If we really put things into a broader perspective, maybe there is no such thing as "bad" karma. It can be thought of as an opportunity to have an experience that will help us grow and understand a better way of being. Good karma may be something as simple as extra peace and love earned, as a result of unconditional love and service lovingly given to others.

Karma (energy that needs to be balanced) can also manifest as love, hate, greed, or other emotions or attitudes. It manifests as the energy that needs to be balanced. If you find yourself in some emotion, such as love or hate, and it seems out of balance or without a good basis, you may wish to check on its source.

Once a person understands the karma behind a situation, much of its power is released and the person is not so caught up in it. Sometimes knowledge of karmic reason is held back until the person has experienced enough so that growth is made.

Not all things that happen to people are from karma. Many times it brings growth, working through genetic things, or as growth for others.

Sources of Karma

Where karma is considered, most people usually think of karma of their own past lives. True, this is a very important aspect of the karmic force. However, a person is always affected by different kinds of karma (see Sources of Karma, Chart 1, page 36).

When two or more karmas coincide with one another, the effect is much harder on a person. However, the growth possible is very great too.

For instance, if a person has been egotistical and self-centered and is born into a family that has a strong genetic tendency towards egotism and self-centeredness, then it will be a much larger problem. Problems become more apparent when they have double sources.

Personal Karma

Some examples of personal karma are:

> *Loving one person to the exclusion of others.* If you've loved one person to the exclusion of others, you will sometime have a life that will block a new relationship with the loved one, forcing you to relate to others.

Personal Karma	This karma is caused by things an individual has done or not done and, therefore, is solely responsible for it. It may have been created through many lifetimes.
Relationship Karma	This involves interactions or non-interactions between two or more persons, which brings imbalance (karma).
Genetic Karma	This is the sum total of unresolved karma present in your cellular structure and put there by ancestors.
Group Karma	It may be political, religious, racial, societal, or some other form. Actions and non-actions affect all members of these groups whether they were intimately involved or not. When you've been a member of a group that has created karma, you are connected with that group until the karma is balanced. You can work it out individually, but it is difficult to do so.
Karma taken on for others	This involves taking over someone else's responsibilities or growth that are that person's opportunities to release karma.

Chart 1. Sources of Karma

Equality. If you've looked down on someone else, you will need to learn to look at that person as your equal. This may happen by first learning to look up to them and at other times forcing yourself to recognize their equality with you. What you least want to give or be towards another may be what you most need to give or be.

Blocking others. If you try through jealousy, envy, or whatever, to hold down another person's growth, you will also hold down your own growth. If you hold back what you have to give them, you will also hold yourself back. Growth comes in sharing one's own growth.

Exchanging energy. One needs to be appreciative of others and willing to return energy to the one giving, whether it be love, money, or some other form. If you are always out looking for something for nothing, you will soon find you are receiving nothing for something.

If you give looking for a return, it may not come the way you think. If you give expecting a return in a certain way, chances are sure that you will not receive in the way you intended. Attaching that kind of pull to a gift twists the energy and the response changes and can become negative.

Preference for location. Previous lives can cause you to choose a particular type of home or area, which was similar to one in a previous life. You may have felt happy in that situation or closer to God, and wish to re-create that energy.

Attitudes. Previous lives can be the cause of "personal sayings" or attitudes. For instance, "I'll always help when I see someone in trouble. I will not run away," or "I'll be careful where I help, I may get taken advantage of," or "Others owe me help."

Choices. Previous lives can affect tastes in clothing, lifestyle, and just about anything where individual tastes apply.

Ego. Everyone needs a healthy ego. It is important to our well-being and opens us to the spiritual levels. In the unhealthy states a person may be egotistical, which brings an overblown ego. This type of person sees himself as the center of everything. A reverse ego is where the person puts himself down and sees no value in the self. A person with ego problems pulls himself into situations to help balance this force.

A person's relationship with his or her Creator, God, is an important part of the ego's development. The following is a meditation that may help in your ego's development.

—Meditation—
Your Creator, God

Be in a meditative state, open to past lives.
   a. Ask to remember or see a past life when your ego got in the way and you had little or no relationship with your Creator, God.
   b. Ask to remember or see a past life when you so totally ignored or blocked your

ego development and were over-depen-
dent on your Creator, God.
  c. How are you doing, this life, in this area?

Inaction. This is the karma of not doing what is there for you to do either through choosing not to or by being oblivious to the opportunity. Sometimes the karma of inaction brings a stronger retribution than the karma of improper action.

—Meditation—
Karma of Inaction

Be in a meditative state, open to past lives.
  a. Ask to remember or see a past life or lives when you refused to act or were oblivious to what you should be doing.
  b. How are you doing, this life, in this area?

Relationships: Situational Karma

Sometimes people come into a relationship because of situational karma. An example is when a person needs to learn to say good-bye or to release another person. Something may have happened that kept them from continuing the relationship in a past life. It could have been death, the other person may have lost interest and found someone else or some other situation may have arisen to end the relationship. Some people find it difficult to let go of grief. It is not noble to spend the remainder of one's life in grief. The griever is held back in her growth. It may be difficult to release someone, but life moves on and we need to go with its flow.

Another karmic reason for a relationship is to fulfill previous life desires to be with one another.

Another situational karmic reason can be to take care of someone during severe trials, illness, or other problems because the person did the same for you in a past life.

If there is not much substance other than karmic in the relationship, the caring for one or need to relate to another can fade away once fulfillment is reached. When this happens one wonders how anything so fulfilling and meaningful could turn to nothing so quickly.

Relationships: Attitudinal Karma

There are many negative attitudes by which a person can create much karma and much pain. One of the biggest negative attitudes is jealousy. The positive side of jealousy is to make you look at what goals or intentions you wish to set. Jealousy is telling you that there is an area of growth or development you need to make. If your mate or date is flirting with someone else, you may need to look at your own behavior—are you playful or flirtatious in the relationship or is this just how the other person is? You have choices. You can either become more playful, flirtatious or lively in the relationship, or you may choose to stay the same and take your chances of the relationship continuing. If you think this person is just the kind that likes to flirt, then again you have several choices. You may decide to work with the person, to sulk, or to get out of the relationship. Whatever decision a person makes should be based on the growth of the persons involved. A relationship that doesn't involve the growth of both persons is usually destined for trouble.

Another negative attitude is control. The less control a person has of herself the more she will try to control her environment, including other people. If you are the one with the control issue, you may want to work on developing inner control, thus freeing up the spontaneity of the relationship. People who are passive can also be very controlling just by their passivity. Sometimes people will get into controlling as part of an ego game. If the other person is excessive in control, you may ask yourself if you are learning to stand up to that kind of energy. Can you match the other person's strength?

Some people like to be controlled, then they do not feel guilty if something goes wrong. If a person does this, he will be in another life where he will be continually forced to make decisions and exercise control in life.

Relationships: Releasing Attachment

If you release and understand whatever was pulling you into a karmic situation with someone and the other person does not, you become free from this attachment, even if the other person has not learned the lesson. You are not stuck with others while they learn unless you wish to continue the relationship. Otherwise, that person will then be attracted to a relationship with someone else where she will have another opportunity to balance the problem.

Importance of Relationships

Relationships are the most important part of life with which we are ever involved. Most important is our relationship to God, which can bring a better balance with others.

We are born in relationship to people and we die in relationships to people whether we admit it or not. Even the hermit is involved through his denial of relationships. Relationships are also probably the most difficult aspects of our lives, and at the same time the most rewarding.

Things to Learn in Relationships

1. Ability to share.

2. Ability to work together.

3. Knowing when to appropriately challenge, encourage, or inspire one another.

4. Being aware of your and the other person's needs in a relationship and how to keep them healthy and reasonable.

5. Being open and truthful to yourself and others in any given situation, remembering this doesn't mean that you have to tell everything you know. Being open and truthful in a relationship allows you to discover new truths.

6. Being yourself. If you have to change your personality or force yourself to be different when you are with someone, it will create incredible tensions and usually bring negative energies.

7. Being fair and respectful with other people whether you can stand them or not.

8. Sharing maintenance duties in a relationship so that you both feel invested in it. This means doing for one another, listening to one another, taking time to be with one another.

9. Don't dump all your problems on the other person and don't let them do it to you.

10. Having the courage to stay with the other person through disagreements and heavy times. Don't run when the going gets rough. Can you imagine what it must have been like for Jesus to sit at the Last Supper knowing that one of His disciples would betray Him and the others fighting over where they would sit with Him in the heaven worlds?

11. Learning to love without attachment, developing unconditional love. This doesn't mean that you have to put up with everything that happens. It means developing a freeing love. A question to ask yourself is "Can I let that person go if that is best for me or that person?"

12. Don't let yourself be mesmerized or controlled by another whether it be a lover, friend, family member, boss, guru or whatever. You are responsible for your own power.

13. Learning to relate from both your heart and your head. Love is not enough. We have responsibilities, destinies to accomplish, which sometimes are ignored because of being too caught up in a relationship.

14. Recognizing that although relationships exist forever on the soul level, in a particular life

they may be short term or long term. If a relationship ends it doesn't mean that you won't see this person again. It just means that it is an end to this chapter. If you stubbornly hang on to all relationships you will hold yourself back.

15. If you are in a relationship with someone, don't wear yourself out trying to figure out the karma or purpose of the relationship. Live and be in the relationship and if at times it becomes very difficult, you may then wish to find out different purposes. Always analyzing interferes with living.

16. Keeping your priorities straight. Remember that you need to love yourself second to the greater power of the universe, and then others as you would yourself.

17. Don't limit your friendships to just one or two persons. We are in a time of expansion and need to relate to many different kinds of people and many different age groups. Isolation may be necessary once in a while, but long term it is not healthy.

18. Don't rush into sex. You can blow your energy out through the sexual areas and end up with a short-lived relationship. It is better to develop as friends first, acquiring a steadiness and depth in the relationship before deciding if you want to make the kind of commitment that includes sex.

19. Learning to see God in others and not see others as God.

20. Learning to really know others as people and not as an extension of yourself.

21. Building a unit, a life together, is the usual purpose of marriage relationships.

22. Don't try to break up friendships between others. If you do, you'll probably be the one left out.

23. Thinking or feeling negatively towards others may be felt either consciously or unconsciously by the other person. It usually results in your being left out of the relationship.

24. When you truly relate with someone on a level of the spirit, you will feel your spirits dancing above your heads.

Genetic Karma

You inherit genetic karma from your ancestors. It may be attitudes, situations, or illnesses. If an ancestor has created a strong imbalance, this can be handed down in the structure of the DNA, causing descendants who are open to this particular thing to come under its karmic influence.

Illness is one of the main karmas that is genetically transmitted and needs to be understood and transformed or it will continue down through the generations until it is played out. In some cases it may thin out from connecting with other genetic streams that have a stronger energy. For instance, if a person has inherited a problem with his or her heart, their children or grandchildren may not have as many problems if they marry into a family that has strong and healthy heart systems. However, it could still surface many generations later.

In changing the genetic pattern a person needs to go back into the past lives of her ancestors who had the problem and work with it from that place. It may be worked in a similar method that the person uses to work out her own current problems. If this is done and the energy pattern of the karma released, it will also help release it from other descendants, since we are all psychically connected to our relatives.

Sometimes people who have created a genetic or family karmic situation may choose to come back into the family in a future generation in order to work on and release that karma. This may apply to many different situations; illness being just one example.

—Meditation—
Genetic Karma

a. *What illness, physical problem or pattern have you inherited?*

b. *Have you created this karma in your family in a previous life or did someone else?*

c. *If you didn't create the problem, what made you want to incarnate into a family with this situation?*

d. *What do you want to hold onto and enhance that is in your genetic stream?*

On a more positive note, many people will reincarnate back into the same family line because they have helped to build a genetic system more attuned to the kind of spiritual growth, creativity, or mental achievement in which they are interested.

Family Curses

Curses put on families or on people were quite common in older times. Nowadays people are more inclined to sue one another. Some curses were almost poetic in their form and delivery. Words and intents have a power of their own and curses actually work. What the curser does not understand, however, is that they come under some of the same effects as whatever they wished on someone else.

Today, curses are not as formal, but when you damn someone or wish them harm, it also has the same effect.

—Meditation—
Family Curses

Be aware of the top of your spinal column in your head. It is a storage place for some of the stronger past life energy in our systems. Open to the energy from that area. While focusing in that area, ask the following questions:

    a. Do you sense a curse has been placed on your family?

    b. Did you put it there in a past life or did someone else?

    c. How has it affected you?

    d. Ask that all negativity from this curse be turned into a positive energy for you and your family.

Examples of family curses include the inability to prosper, problems with children or romances, or an inability to achieve fame.

If you think you or your family is under a curse, ask that its energy be blessed and turned to a positive so that it will benefit you instead. The energy of the curse has been sent to you, therefore, with prayer, blessings and your intent; you can use it however you wish. Some people like to send curses and negative feelings back to the sender. If the person's will and energies are strong enough it can sometimes be done. However, this has a tendency to create more problems, especially since someone back in the family may have done something negative to aggravate the curser into saying the curse!

—Meditation—
Personal Curses

a. *Is there a curse placed on you personally?*

b. *What was the situation when this curse was placed on you? Did you deserve it? Ask for forgiveness for any action you committed that may have helped bring this to you.*

c. *If you don't feel you deserved it, ask that understanding be sent to the curser and, also, let your forgiveness flow to that person.*

d. *Ask that the energy of the curse turn to a positive for you.*

Blessings

Blessings are similar to curses. They are said with direct intent and are meant to affect the person's or family's life. However, they are meant in a positive way.

—Meditation—
Blessings

Be aware in your heart area. Blessings are more likely to affect this area in particular.

　　a. Is there a blessing placed on your family?

　　b. How is it affecting you?

　　c. Could you tap into it and use it more?

　　d. Did you, in a previous life, place this blessing on this family?

　　e. Who placed it on you and what were the circumstances?

　　f. Are you availing yourself of its benefits?

Group Karma

Group karma can include one group or class of citizens forcing its will or ideas on another group. It can be based on religion, politics, or financial philosophies and usually involves control of one or more groups by another. It can include violence or war.

Karma Taken on for Others

Many people in the name of helpfulness will take on projects or fulfill a purpose for someone else, thus depriving that person of needed development of skills or learning. Usually the person who takes it on will quite often feel unappreciated or may find that what he has taken on is more difficult than it needs to be. The difficulty comes from forcing the energy away from the person for whom it was intended.

On the other hand, sometimes it is beneficial for both persons when someone helps or takes on karma for the other person. Knowing when it is all right to help and when it isn't is difficult. If the desire to help comes primarily from the ego, it is usually incorrect. However, if the heart and solar plexus feel involved (but not attached), it may be that it is great to help.

Christ and other highly developed spiritual beings are able to do this and usually transmute the energy to positive. However, if the person doesn't learn from the situation, it may continue to appear until she does learn the lesson.

Creating Karma

Fear of karma can also hold a person back from taking action or learning new things. However, it seems more karma is created by refusing to act and grow than by mistakes that are made.

Some people are so afraid of creating karma or not being spiritual enough that they try to negate their human sides. In a number of regressions into past lives, we've seen persons who actually had achieved very high levels in their spiritual development, but couldn't maintain it because of a lack of human development. This life they were forced by circumstances to deal with the human part of life in order to balance overall growth.

Types of Karma

There are three main types of karma: attitudinal, situational, and karmic drive.

Attitudinal Karma

This relates to attitudes or ways of being that a person carries from life to life. This type permeates all that a person is and all that a person does. Some of the atti-

tudes commonly carried over are egotism, fear of fail-
ure, a sense of not belonging, the "king or queen"
complex, and self-preservation.

These karmic attitudes are usually locked in a person's superficial fascia, which is the area located
under a person's skin. It connects the skin with a
deeper level of fascia, it helps in the flexibility of the
skin and is a pliable area for vessels and nerves. If a
lot of thought forms (energy masses caused by
thoughts) or karmic energy is stored in the fascia, it
makes a person less limber.

—Meditation—
Fascia Blocks

*Be in a meditative state. Focus your awareness on
your superficial fascia (under your skin). Where
does it feel tight or blocked? Send extra energy to
that area to release it. You may also massage the
area. Ask what karmic attitudes are locked in
that area. How can you change those attitudes?*

Situational Karma

This relates to a particular happening from a past life,
which is only activated when a person is around others
involved in the situation. If negative, it may result in
negative behavior that seems to have no basis in the
current life. It feels as though there is a strong push or
desire to do something. It may be to inspire or to help
someone whom you previously held back or to whom
you were negative. Chakras (energy vortices) are excellent places to look for situational karma (see Figure 3,
page 53).

—Meditation—
Balancing Situations

Be in a meditative state. Choose a chakra from Figure 3 with which to work. Focus about six inches out in front of it. Ask to comprehend a situation that you need to balance this life. Let your mind be open and let your thoughts ramble. Usually something comes to your awareness. Watch your thoughts and feelings. You will usually recognize what you need to do about it.

You may repeat the exercise with other chakras. We don't recommend you do this with too many at once.

Karmic Drive

It relates to energies put in motion in a previous life, which seek completion in this life. These forces can relate to any area of life and may be of a positive or negative nature.

Some causes of this type include:

Yearnings – To yearn is to send energy out to an idea, a person, an action, or a possession. A person may have yearned to invent something or share information. The yearning may have been to have a relationship with someone. It may have been to have a certain career or accomplish a particular goal. The yearning energy becomes attached to whatever the object or person is. Sometimes a person is so consumed by the yearnings that the rest of her life, and sometimes even future lives, is affected.

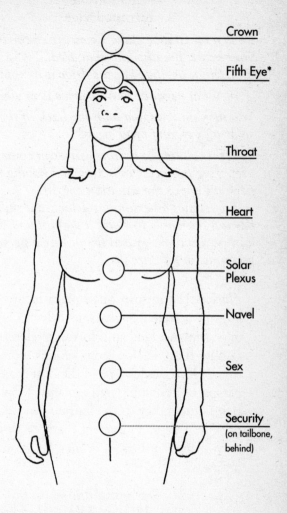

Figure 3. Chakras (energy vortices) are excellent places to look for situational karma (*for further information on the fifth and the other seven eyes, refer to **Kundalini and the Chakras** by Genevieve Lewis Paulson).

—Meditation—
Karmic Drive

Be in a meditative state. Be aware of the back of your heart. Breathe into that area.
  a. What positive karmic drive is in your life?
  b. What negative karmic drive is in your life?
You may do the same with the back of the belly, solar plexus, and head areas.

Other causes of karmic drive can come from preparing for a role or action and having the person's life or the situation cut off.

Sometimes a person has achieved a skill, but has not been able to share it with others. The karmic drive energy can then cause a person to go public in a future life.

Place – The idea of one's place in life can be heavily affected by karmic drive. The place may relate to fame and fortune, relationships, family, lifestyle, location, or any number of things. Karmic drive from the past may help a person by providing extra energy. However, if that extra energy of the karmic drive does not fit with a person's current plans or destiny, it may bring confusion or detract from one's progress.

—Meditation—
Place in Life

Be in a meditative state. Focus about six inches in front of the solar plexus chakra (see Figure 3).
  a. Is there is a karmic drive regarding your place in life which affects that chakra?

b. *Let your thoughts ramble and watch them*
   for information.

Occupation – Hopes and dreams for occupations or careers are sometimes held back by inad-
equacy, fear, or unworthiness, or the person may
have suffered failures so great that the bleedover
or memory holds back attempts towards
achievements in the current life. The reverse is
also true. Memories of good experiences can
help a person achieve more in this life.

—Meditation—
Occupational Forces

Be in a meditative state, open to past lives. Focus
your awareness on your navel, solar plexus, and
center of your forehead.
   a. *Are there past life failures affecting today's*
      success? If so, is there anything you can
      learn from them?
   b. *Fill the navel, solar plexus, and center of*
      forehead with a lavender color to heal old
      memories.
   c. *Are there past life successes that have had a*
      helpful effect on today's career or occupa-
      tion?
   d. *If so, ask that these energies be blessed and*
      help you even more.
   e. *Is there something you are doing or can do*
      to better help forces toward career or occu-
      pation in the future?

Black Holes and Good Clouds

If a person continues to do a certain act or refuses to do something they are destined to do, and this pattern continues over a period of lives, it will have a tendency to create a "black hole" in the person's energy pattern. By black hole we mean a dark spot in one's energy, which has the tendency to pull its owner into similar situations through its force, thus compounding the negative karma.

These "black holes" are caused by the person pulling away from opportunities. The energy that was meant to expand out is literally pulled in and can cause congestion or illness if not worked out.

This can happen through refusal to help others, whether through not sharing, inspiring, loving or through rejecting others.

When you are around this kind of person you will feel shut out or ignored. You may also feel negativity coming from the person. This kind of person may also be heavily prejudiced. Prejudices are excuses for not loving or relating.

If a person dedicates herself to doing good for others and becomes attached to those acts, it, too, can create an imbalance. Also, if the person continually puts others ahead of herself, to the detriment of her own development or completion of a particular life destiny, instead of the black hole this person will create a cloud of good karma. Similar to the black holes' attraction, the cloud will pull the person into situations where she continues to help others with their purposes, to the exclusion of her own. If the person still refuses to balance her giving, she may find her good deeds unwelcome. The intended recipient may feel pressured or be uninterested, thus rejecting the other person's giving. We cannot continue to work only for others' destinies, we also need to work on the destiny given to us. This can also relate to overdoing good deeds.

Eventually this energy will reverse and the person will find her good deeds unwelcome or she may live a life of struggle, which forces her to pay attention to the self.

Granted, there are times when we dedicate a life or lives to service. However, in this case, it was the destiny for that life or lives. When a person's energy is continually building up someone else's parade, they disregard the parade God gave to them.

Sometimes a person will have a life of great illness or trials and tribulations, thus putting him in a position where it is necessary to receive a lot of care and kindness from others. This not only becomes a way to receive the good karma, it also teaches the person to receive from others.

Transmuting Karma

Karmic force in all situations, whether caused by attitudes, feelings, actions, or inactions, must be played out or transmuted. If played out, it means the person will find himself pulled into situations where this energy can be balanced. It may relate to love, anger, sex, business, family, friendship, enemies or any number of ways. If a person daydreams, sometimes he will work out karma in the daydream through understanding and releasing the energy patterns.

Transmuting karma means to change the karmic force into a balanced, pure energy. This usually involves feelings of love and understanding. Christ has enough powerful energies that when a person understands the negativity they've done through a request for forgiveness, they will find the karma balanced. They will need to forgive themselves as well. There are other enlightened beings who have abilities to do the same thing.

Karma simply means that for every action there is a reaction. If something happens to you, you can simply dismiss it as, "it's my karma, I have to take it," or you can look at the action. Perhaps you cannot stop the action from happening, but you, with your free will, have the opportunity of reacting, or not reacting to it as you choose. Some karmic incidents repeat themselves over and over again. As one person does an unkindness to another, the second person returns it. The first person does it again. It is much like a game of tennis, which does not end when a certain score is reached. Rather it ends only when one of the persons involved decides they have had enough of such action and reacts in a different way or else transmutes the energy into a pure releasing love. It may also be likened to a wheel that continues to go around.

When the wheel of karma runs over a person, the person will attract behavior from other people and situations, which will make her aware of things to work out. There may be a tendency to blame someone else for the problem when actually it is the person herself who is attracting the behavior or situation. Karma that is refused or ignored becomes stronger and usually more negative each time it appears until it is so powerful that a person can no longer ignore it.

Perhaps someone has done something to you that was not karmic in nature, but comes from that person's inability to live life with love. You can return the action karmically, either in this life or in another, or you can release them in love.

There are three main steps in releasing or working through karma.

The first step is to be aware of what we are doing. The second step is to make choices. The third step is to change and actually live the choices.

For example, if a person realizes that the energies in a particular situation do not make sense to him, then a past life karma is probably involved. The first step then is for him to be aware of whether or not his involvement is out of proportion or inappropriate.

The second step is to understand what other choices for actions, attitudes or feelings are involved and which ones should be released and which ones more fully explored.

The third step is to then follow through and make the changes. Sometimes a person finds that immediate release of tension or problems happen. Other times people may find that steps two and three should be reviewed and perhaps replaced.

—Meditation—
Karma Releasing

Be aware of a situation in life that doesn't make good sense to you.

> *a. Let your shoulders relax and be in a meditative state.*

> b. *What is the bigger picture of the situation, and what choices are open? Take some time to explore the choices and then see which one or ones feel best to you.*
>
> c. *Imagine yourself changing and actually living the new choices.*
>
> d. *Take some action to help bring the new energies and new way of being into you.*

Dealing with Karma

Karma makes sure we keep on the right path of evolution. It may seem to slow us down sometimes, but it does fill in the gaps of learning so that we have a better base for further evolution.

It's almost impossible not to gather some karma along the way and we need not make too big a deal of it. It is just what happens. As water seeks its level, so do energies seek to find their own level or balance. The following are some ways to help achieve this balance.

1. When you don't understand something, open your heart chakra area (see Figure 3) and gently let energy flow out. Let go of what you are feeling and let deeper feelings come through. Sometimes wonderful new perceptions come through.

—Meditation—
Opening the Heart Chakra for Understanding

Be in a meditative state. Open your heart chakra and ask what you need to understand.

2. If someone "pushes your buttons," change your energy pattern so you are not caught in it. Deep breathing, balancing energies in and around your body, changing the subject (if you can), or just leaving the area can help. Sometimes it is helpful to push back. However, that can escalate problems also. When you are by yourself, do the following meditation to see why you had a strong reaction.

—Meditation—
Exaggerating Feelings

Be in a meditative state. Re-experience the feeling of having "your buttons pushed." Breathe into any area of your body that strongly reacted. Exaggerate the feelings so you can be aware of what's behind your reaction. Usually looking at the behind-the-scenes information releases the negativity.

3. Recognize that agreement is sometimes not possible and suggest that you and the other person(s) "agree to disagree."

—Meditation—
Agreeing to Disagree

Be in a meditative state. In what areas of your life do you need to agree to disagree?

4. Learn what are good boundaries for yourself. We are coming into a more enlightened age when it is more recognized that everyone has

the right to his or her own thoughts, feelings, and actions. Suppression and repression of others or of yourself are not in keeping with the new expanding energies.

—Meditation—
Boundaries

Be in a meditative state.
  a. *Where are your boundaries not defined?*
  b. *Where do you not pay attention to your own boundaries?*
  c. *Where are you not aware of someone else's boundaries?*

5. Be careful not to put others down or you may pull the same situation in on yourself so that you will learn what it's really like.

—Meditation—
Non-Critical

Be in a meditative state. Are you being critical of someone else? Do you need a deeper understanding of what he is going through? What can you do to improve your own situation?

6. Don't push what won't go.

—Meditation—
Blocking by Pushing

Be in a meditative state. Sometimes we try so hard to get something done or to happen only to find that something better is trying to manifest itself.

a. *What are you pushing that won't go? Can you let loose of it?*

b. *What are you blocking by your desire for something else?*

7. Don't make mountains out of molehills or molehills out of mountains.

—Meditation—
Mountains vs. Molehills

Be in a meditative state.
a. *What are you trying to make bigger than it needs to be?*

b. *What are you denying or ignoring?*

8. Balance thoughts and feelings. When you do, actions are usually more appropriate and effective.

—Meditation—
Aligning Thoughts, Feelings, Actions

Be in a meditative state.
a. *Where are your thoughts and feelings in disagreement?*

b. *Is there a situation where you are saying one thing and feeling another?*

9. Remember if you feel good about and respect yourself, you are more likely to attract that from others. However, if you are very egotistical you may attract the opposite reactions.

—Meditation—
Attracting Reactions from Others

Be in a meditative state. Feel good about your-self and how you are working with your life. Let those feelings permeate your entire body. This can help give courage and inspiration to do more or be more!

10. Periodically in your meditations ask what there is to balance today.

—Meditation—
Daily Balancing

Be in a meditative state. Ask what you could bal-ance today. If nothing comes right away, let your mind ramble. Usually a number of things come to one's awareness.

11. Karma and problems can come from not acting when you should.

—Meditation—
Karma or Action

Be in a meditative state. Ask what actions you need to take today that will help prevent karma.

12. When things seem strange or negative, ask that all that comes to you turn to good and all that goes from you turn to good as well.

Consciously Creating Karma

If a person wants to achieve a certain thing, it can be helped by consciously creating karma—that means building up an energy that can be balanced by manifesting. This can be done by creating intent through one's feelings and desires. People do this all the time, however, they are not usually aware of the process. It can be helpful to understand this process so you can consciously choose what you want to build up.

For instance, if a person wanted to be a teacher, she must:

1. Have the desire. Interestingly enough, the person may not even recognize or admit to herself that this is so. Recognizing and acknowledging the desire helps increase its energy.

2. The person's actions must be conducive to the fruition of the goal.

Doing steps one and two creates an energy force that will somehow manifest itself. If the person's genetic makeup, astrological energy, and divine purpose are in accord with the desired goal, then it will likely manifest this life.

However, if compatible energy is lacking in the genetic makeup, the astrological force or divine purpose, then the fruition will happen during a future life. For instance, a slightly built person with a weak body may have trouble trying to be a sumo wrestler or if the person's astrological energy favors mental and spiritual development rather than physical, that, too, will hold back manifestation. Of course, if the person's destiny energy this life is totally different, that, too, would delay fruition of that particular goal.

Many times people will be doing certain things that seemingly have no relevance to their current life. These actions are probably from past life desires.

Following are some meditations to help you explore this area:

—Meditation #1—
Discovering Past Life Desires/Goals

Be in a meditative state, as deeply relaxed as possible.

   a. Ask to know of a desire from a past life which you are currently working on in this life.

   b. Do you want to continue it or transmute it?

   c. Do you wish to continue it and even enhance it? Tune into the energy of the desire/goal. Really acknowledge it. Feel it in your body. Breathe into the area where it is located and empower the energies with your breath. Filling your entire body with the energies of this desire/goal can also enhance it.

   d. If you don't want to continue giving energy to the desire/goal, think of some other way you may wish to use the energy. For instance, if you have a desire to be rich and famous and it doesn't seem to be getting you any place, you may wish to change the desire to have plenty and use it wisely, and to fulfill your potential, making the investment of this life really "pay off." When you

*decide what you want to transmute and
where the energy should go, you may really
feel the old desire and with your thoughts
and feelings transmute it by changing the
thoughts into the new desire/goal. Feel that
all over your body and empower it with
your breath.*

—Meditation #2—
New Desires

a. If there is a new desire/goal you wish to
introduce into your manifestation energy
write it down and really look at the word so
you are clear on it. Remember you are creating a karmic drive.

b. Feel the desire/goal in the area behind and
above the solar plexus (destiny/purpose
area). Does it resonate in this area? If so,
you know there will be energy for manifesting from here.

c. Feel the desire/goal mainly in the lower back
of the head (where astrological force comes
in), but also around the entire head. Ask if it
resonates with astrological force. You may
also ask a good astrologer to check your
astrology chart and see if it supports this
endeavor.

d. There are several ways of checking genetic
tendencies.

1. Have any of your ancestors done this or
similar things?

2. Feel the desire/goal all over your body. If
your body supports this endeavor, it will

> *feel good and expansive. There may even be excitement. If your body does not support it, you will feel it pull back or tighten up. If this happens, take the desire/goal out of it.*

For maximum help with the new desire/goal, it really needs the blessings of all three areas. Lastly, you can think about it and bring it into the light of reason. This can help you to formulate plans. If you do the mental first, usually it throws up blocks. Working with energies this way is a part of conscious evolution, where you choose to work with energies. Too often people are into unconscious evolution and find themselves pushed or pulled in confusing ways.

Chapter V

REINCARNATION AND RELATIONSHIPS

WE ARE NOT BORN ALONE, nor do we live or die alone. It may feel or appear that way sometimes, however, there are greater connections with others than most people ever realize. We are part of a greater connectedness beyond the personal relationships with which we are so familiar. We will begin this chapter by first exploring the greater connections.

Soul Relationships: Soul Mates

When people refer to soul mates, they are usually meaning sex mates, someone with whom they can have a powerful sexual-love relationship. True soul mates, however, don't always mate in a life. Many times they are not that interested in the sexual aspect of the relationship. In a true soul mate connection the energy is very powerful and they will help one another expand to new levels. Many times soul mates will be acquainted with one another for a short period of time or a few years with the sole purpose of expanding their growth through the intensity of their energies. They will almost always be the opposite sex in order to balance polarities. However, in any given life, the male and female roles may be the opposite. Soul mates meet a lot on higher planes during sleep and maintain some kind of connection on those levels.

When soul mates are in physical bodies and interacting it can be very difficult. If one person has developed more than the other, then the undeveloped areas of the less developed become an irritant to the more developed person. A person who has developed less of their energies will feel over-challenged.

Perfect Pattern of the Self

There is an energy area in our bodies behind the xiphoid process (the bony appendage at the end of the breastbone) which relates to who we really are. It can be called "the seed of the self" or the perfect pattern of the self that we are to become. Therefore, destiny energies are prevalent in this area (see Figure 4).

When deeply relating to others, your perfect pattern of the self relating to that area in the other person brings more of a soul connection and also a sense that each is an individual soul. It usually brings more clarity in the relationship as well.

When a person is around his or her soul mate this area usually resonates.

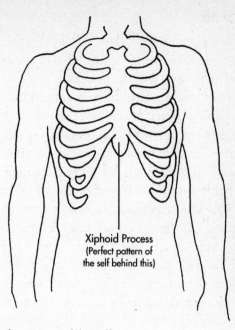

Xiphoid Process
(Perfect pattern of
the self behind this)

Figure 4. Perfect Pattern of the Self

—Meditation—
Connecting with Soul Mates

Be in a meditative state.

    a. Focus on the area behind your xiphoid process. Let yourself be in touch with the energy of who you really are.

    b. Then ask to feel the energy of your soul mate. Do you know this person in this life?

    c. Are you ahead in growth or is your soul mate ahead?

    d. Ask to feel a balance and connection between you and your soul mate. Ask that enlightened peace fill you both.

Twin Souls

Twin souls are very similar and usually the same sex. Sometimes their astrological charts are so closely aligned that they will do the same thing at the same time. They might not even be aware of the other person for many years. If one twin develops and grows, the other twin's growth is automatically enhanced.

There is usually a strong past-life connection with twin souls and they may have gone through a number of difficult situations together, thus building a trust level. When these persons meet, they immediately have a common trust and a common understanding. If they are women, they may find that their kitchens, cupboards, and closets are arranged in very similar manners. The organization of their lives would be similar. For both men and women careers may be remarkably similar and, at times, identical. When men have twin soul relationships, both of their careers and the way they work will have predominant similarities.

—Meditation—
Connecting with Your Twin Soul

Be in a meditative state.
   a. Do you have a twin soul?

   b. What is your twin soul doing?

   c. Who is having a better time with this life pattern—you or your soul twin?

   d. Feel a balance between the both of you and ask that it be filled with enlightened peace.

Soul Families

A soul family can be made up of several thousands of people. You will reincarnate over and over with these souls, sometimes in gentle supportive relationships and sometimes in very intense learning relationships. You will learn to be father, mother, sister, brother, child, as well as any other form of relationship, including lovers or spouses. The ultimate here is that you learn to relate to everyone else from all aspects of relationships. Therefore, you will find that your parents have been your children or your siblings or you may have been married to one another in previous lives. It is similar to children playing house. "It is my turn to be the mamma today," or "my turn to be the child," or "the spouse."

This type of filling all roles with one another includes teaching, being in positions of control or master-servant relationships; in short, any type of relationship possible is worked out in the soul family over and over until we develop strong universal and soul level connections with each other. We learn to experience and share many forms of love.

In this situation if any person or persons hold back on their growth, they hold back the entire soul family. If one person does tremendous amounts of growth they benefit the overall soul family energy, thus affecting each person.

Sometimes members of an older and wiser tribe start out in one incarnation in the same family, then move out to other families or tribes in an effort to help them progress. They may have little or no contact with their own group for the rest of this incarnation, but will get back together in a subsequent incarnation to work on their mutual growth, having completed their "missionary" incarnation. While the efforts made during a "missionary" incarnation do not seem to aid family members, the benefit to humanity improves the growth of all inside and outside the immediate family group. During this incarnation the "missionary" may feel out of place, or as a foreigner in his new family, yet have the sense of purpose and know it is right to be there.

Soul Groups

In soul groups the participants will have an extra agenda whether it is in a leadership role, developing spiritual awareness, or some other form of group activity. Their purpose is to speed the evolution of the people on the planet. Many times these groups develop incredible karma among themselves, which has to be worked out before they can truly work together as a unit. These groups in one lifetime may be in governmental roles, another lifetime in the entertainment business, and still another lifetime in the educational system. They may also spend some lives in military capacities. Their primary focus is the development of others, their own development is secondary.

Many of these people originated on other planets and although they will interact with soul families and soul tribes, their main function is with the soul group.

Soul Tribes

Soul tribes consist of a number of soul families that may vary from tribe to tribe. One of their main functions is propagation of particular abilities or talents.

Most of our lives are lived in relationships—good, bad or indifferent. We are born helpless and totally dependent on others for care. Some people live the same way before death. My uncle, who experienced a long illness and weakness before death, said, "So often persons are babies twice in their life, at the beginning and at the end." We learn to receive by being in a dependent state and learn compassion and giving by taking care of the dependent ones.

Interdependence is definitely a part of our lives in so many ways. There are the usual stages of relating, dependent as a baby, child, teenager, youth, middle and old age. However, there are also awareness stages we go through that have nothing to do with the age. This awareness deals with responsibility and is something we will learn and experience in many different ways.

Past Life Ties

Everyone with whom we interact in a meaningful way, whether positively or negatively, has ties with us from a previous life or lives. Understanding the dynamics of the tie can help break through many problems and bring enrichment into the interactions.

Chapter VI
AKASHIC RECORDS

AKASHA IS A SANSKRIT TERM that refers to a primordial substance upon which is imprinted the events of
our lives.

The information imprinted on the akasha includes
your actions, desires, hopes, dreams, all of your life
and your reactions to it. This includes past lives, what
they were and what they are destined to be; the present as it is and as it is destined to be. It also includes
the probable futures that you have and the destiny
purposes for them. The records also contain information regarding the overall evolution of the person.

These records are three-dimensional. Usually the
records are viewed in two dimensions as one would
watch a VCR. There is up and down and sideways.
However, greater depth in viewing these records
brings a third dimension and shows there are also

events happening "behind" the action. This is similar to the background scenes shown of any action, however, it involves an even bigger picture. These other background areas include the energy of the family, community, religion, race, country. There is also a thread or line of continuity that underlies the akashic records connecting all lives and the time spent between lives. It is this line continuity that contains all information, what's learned, what needs to be balanced karmically, and the underlying personality of the person.

Each person has his or her own record. It contains pictures that show actions, convey feelings and reveal all energies of that life. It also shows things that should have been done but weren't. These uncompleted things then attach themselves to the line of continuity of lives and will "haunt" persons until there is a completion.

These records can be viewed through meditative, psychic, or intuitional states. Information sometimes appears in dreams. You can fast forward, reverse, stop or continue the viewing of the records as well as enhance their energies to sense them more deeply.

Colors

Some scenes of the akashic records when viewed will show clear, bright, vivid colors as though it's happening now. This indicates that this particular part of life was lived in depth, or to the fullest. Great awareness was achieved during this period. If the life is lived without much awareness, there will be a sepia colored background.

At other times there is an overriding background of color that relates to the energies the person is working with. Events that have soft pastels indicate completion of karma or growth. There is a spiritual connection with them. Sometimes there is a dark purple background for past scenes, sometimes there is a burnished gold background indicating future scenes.

Bleedover

At times during our evolutionary progress, certain situations or attitudes will imprint themselves, or rather, we will, by our extra energy directed to the occurrence, imprint these particular situations on our akashic records in a deeper way. It is much like a film that overdevelops one part of the picture. This causes what could be called "bleeding" of these particular instances or attitudes into other lives.

This means the power in these events affect future lives. For instance, if a person drowns with great fear and horror, he will in the future have a fear of water or a fear of drowning. However, if a person willingly accepts the death, there is no bleedover.

These instances would not be what could be called karmic in the usual sense of the word, but nevertheless, by their force, they may affect many future lives and continue to affect them until the person becomes aware of the deep imprint, and by one means or another releases the deep imprint. In these cases, it is a release of the bleedover that balances one's energy.

Some of the deep imprints, or overexposures, can only be released by living through countless numbers of lives until the bleedover fades away. Other times, through extraordinary happenings, the person may become aware and thus release the incidents. Another way is through understanding gained from regressions into past lives.

Attachment

Being too attached to people or things will cause an overlay or cloud the akashic records. Watching too much television or generally being more of a spectator than a participant in life can weaken the life force so that positive imprints are not made on the records. It's as though the purpose of some lives will have to be repeated at a later time since not enough energy was expended to matter.

Fantasy Life

Sometimes there is an overlay of actual events, which represents a person's fantasy of their life. When an event is too difficult to handle, a person may imagine that it was different from what it was. This imagination forms the overlay that some day must be removed either through past life awareness or through recognition of the reality in a later event which is similar. If this is done it helps release the earlier one.

For instance, if a person has a life where she thinks that she was highly successful or greatly loved when the opposite was true, then either in that life or in a future life she will have to see situations more clearly. She will need to recognize that her view is not accurate. It may be a painful lesson to learn.

The reverse is also true. A person may be down on himself, feeling or thinking that he has no self-worth or achievements when the reverse was actually true. He will sometime have to recognize and appreciate his accomplishments.

The interesting thing in the reincarnation process is that qualities such as love, steadfastness, endurance, understanding, empowering of self and others, goodness, control of energies that affect the self, and being in tune with a greater power count more in the overall development than in stature achieved in human eyes. For instance, a person who has learned to love unconditionally and in a healthy non-attached manner may have achieved as much or more growth as someone who ruled a country or invented helpful things. We say "may" as we can't truly judge what people do learn and do gain in their lives. We need to remember, however, that qualities can continue into future lives, even if accomplishments do not.

Obtaining Akashic Record Information

There are many ways that a person can receive information from the past. Some are:

1. Induced regressions. These may be guided by self or others, in full consciousness or through hypnosis. A person usually goes inward during these. (You may see actual events or symbols of events.)

2. Spontaneous regression. This happens at any time and has a tendency to take over the person's consciousness, usually for a short time.

3. Spontaneous scene changes. In this situation the entire room or area changes and a past life

scene fills the area. The person experiencing this may feel changes as well as be a part of the scene.

4. A scene may appear separately from the person. This, too, is superimposed over the normal area. This also happens when a person sees a past life face over someone's current face or there may be vague impressions of other scenes appearing.

5. Others may see or sense your past lives.

6. Dreams quite often contain past life information. Dreaming of a different time period may indicate a past life.

7. Some astrologers are able to sense past lives based on planetary configurations.

8. Psychic or intuitive impressions.

9. Interpreting behavior, preferences, or hatreds that seemingly have no basis in this life.

10. Asking yourself questions or having others ask you questions. Answers can seem to appear from "nowhere."

Our lives are like a hologram and although our attention may be focused on one area, with our intent we can change our focus to another area. This allows us to experience different areas in consciousness. The more a person's consciousness is developed, not only can she access the past and future better, she can also see into the present at a deeper level.

Changing the Records

The akashic records are not unchangeable. They can be changed. In fact, they are continually affected by what we do and what we learn.

When a person relives a past life, the understanding and growth developed through the years and lives can bring even greater changes. Physical events themselves can't be changed, but the emotions, attitudes, intents, and thoughts can all be affected.

It can also affect actions or events that have not yet happened.

Any time you make a change, not only are your energy patterns shifted, but energies of other people who were affected by the change will also be modified. Taking it further, anyone else affected by these other people will also have changes happen within themselves. It could actually affect thousands of people. Also, as others make changes in their lives, you may be affected.

Viewing Akashic Records

The following are some meditations that may be helpful to you in understanding and working with this energy:

Be in a peaceful, relaxed position, with your back straight. Lying down may facilitate the meditations as the body is in a more contemplative state.

—Meditation #1—
Viewing the Akashic Records

Massage the center of your forehead and open that area, letting energy gently flow from it. Get into the feeling of floating and sinking into the

*floor at the same time. This brings a dual aware-
ness that will help you retain your present day
consciousness at the same time you view the
akashic records.*

*Fill your body with an indigo or dark purple
color. Feel your consciousness open up. Ask to
view the record through the center of your forehead. At the same time open an awareness in the
body so that you can feel the energy as well.*

*Watch any picture you may see and pay atten-
tion to any feelings that may arise. Don't judge
them as that will bring you out of the experience. You may judge them when you have completed the viewing. Let yourself be totally
involved in the experience while it is happening
so that you get optimum information and understanding from it.*

*Although some people actually see scenes,
others may sense or feel the actions. Sensing and
feeling will, many times, give greater understanding of the events.*

> *a. Ask the akashic records to show you a
>   specific event or relationship in which you
>   are interested.*
>
> *b. You may ask the records to show you
>   something from the past that is of great
>   importance to you in your life now.*

*When you have finished you may wish to
make notes so that you can refer to them later.
Sometimes more information comes weeks,
months, or years afterwards.*

*Stretch well and move around so that you
fully get back to the present-day consciousness.*

—Meditation #2—
Developing Awareness of Imprinting of Records

Put your consciousness in the center of your forehead, the top of your head, behind the end of the breastbone, and behind the navel. Sit quietly or lie down for a while as these areas receive your attention. Ask what you are currently imprinting on your records in the akasha. Let messages, thoughts, or feelings form. Give them plenty of time to come to your consciousness.

Then stretch well and again move around. Make notes.

—Meditation #3—
Changing the Imprints

Be in a meditative state.

a. *Focus on the center of your forehead and behind the xiphoid process.*

b. *Think of someone with whom you don't have as good a relationship as you would like.*

c. *Ask to see or sense a past life that has bearing on the current situation. What learning do you get from it? What responsibility do you have in the situation?*

d. *Ask for or send forgiveness, whichever is appropriate. Fill yourself and the situation with lavender and love for healing and blessing.*

Akashic Records of the Future

Each time you do something, or think or feel something, you are sending imprints to your probable futures. Yearnings and dreams not fulfilled in this life, or fears not worked out in this life all imprint themselves on the future.

—Meditation—
Imprinting the Future

Be in a meditative state.
> *a. Focus on your solar plexus and center of your forehead.*
>
> *b. Ask how you are imprinting the akashic records in positive ways for the future.*
>
> *c. Ask how you are imprinting the akashic records in negative ways for the future.*
>
> *d. You may make changes by recognizing patterns you don't want and replacing them with a more productive energy.*

Memories of the Future

Our bodies and subconscious know more than we do sometimes. They seem to sense what may happen in the future and what memories the event will bring. If it is unpleasant, the body or subconscious may try to block the event from happening. If pleasant, the body and subconscious will be more open.

People who are afraid of success may find in self-discovery that they block things well in advance of achievement or they may find out when it's too late to change their ways.

—Meditation—
Checking Your Subconscious

Be in a meditative state.

   a. *Tune into your body, especially the navel and belly area. Breathe into the area.*

   b. *Ask what it knows about the future that you don't.*

   c. *Is it helping or hindering manifestation of future things?*

   d. *Negotiate with your subconscious if you need to.*

Recognizing that all of life lived today, or blocked today, imprints the future as well as the present can overload our sense of responsibility. We need to remember that trying too hard is not necessarily appropriate either. Filling ourselves with joy and love as well as other good qualities helps change all our actions into effective ones and helps reduce any tendency to worry.

Certainly we need to be aware of the process, but worrying too much about the future limits how well we can live today.

Chapter VII

REGRESSIONS

ALL THAT YOU'VE LEARNED or done in past lives is still with you. Some of it is buried deep within the akashic energy of your lives and some is very accessible and usable. Going on regressions helps to:

1. Understand abilities and talents from previous lives and bring them to this life if appropriate.

2. Develop better relationships through understanding previous connections.

3. Get a sense of being eternal, thus giving this life more importance.

4. Understand the current life better.

5. Release blocked energies.

6. Become aware of attitudes that may enhance or hold back this life.

7. Overcome fears (death, water, etc.).

8. Understand bleedover (the energies of strong events without resolution, which can run into or bleed over into other situations).

9. Experience other awarenesses and ways of being.

10. Research things from the past.

In regressions people feel a real "me" in the past incarnations and a sense that this "me" is eternal. Situations are different, the bodies are different (one short lady marveled over the feeling of being tall when she experienced a past life as a Portuguese soldier). However, the sense of the individuality continuing is comforting even if the life situations past or present are difficult.

Reactions to Regressions

Some regressions (without hypnosis) have given people beautiful insights into themselves, sometimes painful, sometimes joyful, but always beautiful when it brings deeper, clearer understanding. Other regressions have been interesting and helpful in varying degrees.

When someone else reads your past lives, there may be helpful information, but the information usually does not have the deep meaning for a person that experiencing the regression has. This allows people to re-experience events themselves, reliving their emotions and being aware of their thoughts at that time, but also be aware of their present reactions. It is a dual awareness, an awareness both of the previous life and of what is going on in the present. Hypnosis can be helpful and people sometimes remember the regression, but the feelings and experience usually are not as deep.

It is always a joy to see some of the changes that have been made possible by regressions. The following are some of the reactions that people have shared. H. J. writes:

"My regressions have given me a general feeling of calm, feeling part of the flow of continual progress toward God unity. There is a feeling of contentment that events are going according to divine plan. The regressions have been a great help in understanding reasons for family situations (rebellious child) and how to prevent a repeat of mistakes in this life. It's been a help in knowing there has been a good relationship with my husband previously and learning ways we can work together again in this life. I also received help in understanding any one personality.

"My concept of written law has changed and I realize universal law should be my guide as well. I realize I can't make decisions for others or control them, and have been giving children more freedom. While I never did fear death I wish everyone could re-experience such a lovely one as I did, no one then would fear it. The regressions were a great help to me in meeting karma constructively."

W. M. writes: "Since learning about my past lives, I have had a better understanding of myself in this life. I am able to accept myself as I am and have an understanding of why I am this way. Now that I feel much freer there is a sense of being able to live for myself and for today rather than living in the past. The great feeling of loneliness which I have always carried with me is not as much of a burden as it has been. I understand the source of the loneliness and the reason I will always carry it with me. This helps ease the load. I feel I am much more tolerant of other people. I find it is easier to be with others. I have a greater sense of caring for other people, and I am less apt to condemn people for the things they do or what they are. I do not judge as critically and therefore feel less judged by others."

S. K. writes: "Since receiving a past-life reading for myself, many things have changed. I feel as if a fog has lifted or a thin curtain was pushed aside. Life has taken on a newer, richer meaning for me. Instead of living confusedly from day to day, I can see my path in life clearly and understand the purpose of life and living. I now enjoy things for what they really are, rather than worrying about minute, meaningless details.

"Through a more complete understanding of myself, people's problems are easier to sympathize with, and oftentimes I can help, now that I can 'place' myself in their situation. Whenever I am depressed or disappointed by something, I 'sit' myself down and have an 'inner discussion.' Knowing who I am allows me to use self-analysis, in other words, to reason with my unhappy feelings and understand why I reacted in that way. By applying lessons learned in past lives, I am able to avoid repeating most of the mistakes in this life.

"The fear of death is no longer existent within me, the doctrines preached by many churches never fully satisfied my fears. Their interpretations left me cold and uneasy, because they didn't seem right. I felt there had to be much more than merely non-existence. Otherwise our lives would be totally meaningless.

"It has now been seven months since the regression and it still has a lot of influence on my daily living. I know why I fear heights and feel strong enough to overcome most of it. I know why my sons react to certain things (they also had regressions) and will probably be able to raise them to be kind, caring adults. I know why my husband reacts certain ways to different situations. Our relationship is beautiful and enriching because of this deeper understanding between us. I know now that when death is very near to me, I will look on it as a beginning rather than an end to life. I will know that it is time for my soul to rest until the time is right to be reborn, and the house in which it is enclosed will be laid aside for another.

"It is easier to forgive people and my outlook is more tolerant and loving. It is now a real joy to me when I can help or enlighten someone in any way possible. Life seems to be deeper and richer and yet—simpler!"

Philosophic expansion seems to be one of the greatest changes people experience. They gain a much larger concept of life and the possibilities that bring greater peace and understanding.

Who Should Go on Regressions

Regression therapy seems to be on the increase especially when people cannot seem to find reasons in this life for their concerns or problems. Regressions also give more meaning to many people's lives. The following are some reasons people go on regressions:

1. Those having recurring visions, dreams, fears or negative attitudes which do not seem to have origination in the current life usually benefit greatly.

2. A desire to experience a greater self or wanting to expand their sense of life and lives.

3. Those wishing to overcome a fear of death.

4. Discovering reasons for relationship problems.

5. Curiosity.

Looking for ego aggrandizement is not a great reason for doing a life regression. Most people will find rather normal lives anyway.

Accessing Past Lives

Almost anyone can experience regressing to a past life. Some find it easy the very first time they try. Others may find it takes a second or third time before they really get their awareness into it. So don't be discouraged if you don't feel you get there the first time. Some of you will, and may be very surprised you did it so easily.

There are two ways of checking the akashic records. One is viewing and the other is experiencing.

When viewing the records it is similar to watching a VCR. You can fast forward, reverse or stop the "tape" as well as let it run its natural speed. When viewing the records, a person is watching the action.

In the second method of checking the records, you can put yourself into the body you had previously by expanding your consciousness into your previous body. Then you will be able to experience the emotions, thoughts, attitudes, and the force of the energies within "you." It is the preferable way to obtain information and understanding. It is also a way of releasing some of the energies previously put into your records.

Open Mind

Keep an open mind when you go on regressions. What you see or experience may be totally different from what you imagine. The lives also may seem rather mundane. People who are looking to be great well-known persons with very high development may be disappointed. People who have done very well before probably won't be reincarnating any more.

You will have been in many different situations—rich, poor, good, bad, effective, messed up, good, looking or ugly. It is necessary as part of growth to experience all things.

You may feel as though you are making things up at first. Practice will help you recognize the difference. Also, do not judge or pick apart what you are getting as that will bring you out of it. You can judge and pick apart all you want afterwards.

Preparing for a Regression

Preparation is very important whether you plan to take yourself on the journey or have someone else take you. Following are some things that may enhance the experience:

1. Don't have others (except a leader or facilitator if you have one) in the room. Even if they are quiet and only listening, their vibrations can affect you.

2. Be in a comfortable position. Usually lying down with no pillow is best.

3. Light and noises shouldn't be distracting.

4. Pray for protection, guidance, and clarity.

5. You may wish to record the experience on a tape recorder.

6. You may wish to have paper and pen handy to make additional notes afterward. Also, you may "see" more of these lives in days, weeks, months, or even years later. It is great to include that with your notes for additional information.

7. Don't push or stop the experience. Let information appear to you. If it fades, breathe deeper, but peacefully. Heavy breathing can bring you out of it.

8. Massage your eyebrows well. This helps you focus inwardly.

9. Have a list of questions to ask yourself or if someone is guiding you, she or he can ask your questions.

Those questions can include:

a. How does that body feel compared to today's body?

b. What were you learning in the situation?

c. Is there anything left over to balance this life (karma to complete)?

d. Are there blessings for this life?

e. Any talents, abilities, or insights that can help this life?

f. Anyone from the current life in that life with you?

g. Are there feelings from that life to which you should pay particular attention?

h. Is this a life in which you would like to go through the death you had then?
   (It's best to have guidance on this one. It usually makes it easier to stay with it.)

10. Some things you may wish to remember:

a. If you feel stuck, ask to go ahead in time. It can be hours, days, months, or years.

b. If you feel scared, put the palms of your hands over your solar plexus and breathe into that area.

c. Know that if something is too scary to experience or deal with, you may fill yourself with lavender to heal the vibration. Also, fill yourself with forgiveness, love, and blessings. This will help heal the situation whether or not you understand it.

d. Sometimes you will feel as though nothing is going on. It may be that you have entered a between-lives rest period or you may be spending some time in the area for lost souls. This area is a darkish gray and a person feels suspended and not able to make contact with others. Time spent in this area is usually a result of the previous life being lived in a very self-centered way or in an almost hermit-like existence. We are meant to relate as part of our growth.

If you find yourself here, forgive yourself and ask to be in the light. You may also move forward to another time.

e. Don't hassle yourself when you see less than perfect existences. We all have them. It's what you can learn from them that is important. Even more important is when you act on that learning.

What to Do during the Regression

1. Don't try too hard. It brings you into too strong a mental mode. You will want to be in a higher state of consciousness beyond time and space. Pretending you don't care if you get anything or not brings a more open, receptive state.

2. Know that sensing, seeing, or perceiving are all valid.

3. *Focus* more on your body than your head, especially the belly area and back. Let your mind ramble so the information can better come to your awareness.

4. Choose a focus or visualization to use beforehand. This becomes your trigger to resonate with and unlock the memories from the akashic records. When you choose a visualization, imagine it while you are breathing into it and memory should surface.

   Some examples of things to visualize are:
   a. Color.

   b. Walking down a path.

   c. Standing by water.

   d. Holding something.

   e. Seeing or being on an old ship.

   f. Sitting.

   g. An emotional quality—see yourself as joyful, sad, excited, or some other strong emotion.

5. When you visualize something and breathe into the visualization, you create a vibration or resonance, which can attract a past life that relates to that vibration. On occasion, it may trigger a future life experience instead.

   Areas you may wish to focus on are:
   a. A particular chakra.

b. The area between the pineal and pituitary glands (see Figure 5 below).

(It's best to have someone with you when you do this one as rather violent or negative past lives can come from this area.)

c. Navel and belly area. This puts you in touch with your subconscious, which can be referred to as the first consciousness (combination of the physical and the emotional).

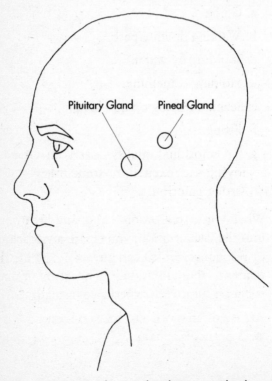

Figure 5. Between the Pineal and Pituitary Glands

    d. An illness or injury.

    e. Relationships.

    f. Facets of a career.

    g. Dance movements. If you use music from past centuries or other cultures and allow your body to dance as it will, past life memories many times appear.

6. If you feel you are only in a fantasy you may be! Usually you can go into the reality by breathing deeper, focusing more closely on your body and asking to see the life as it was.

7. If you are crying and can't work through it, exaggerate the crying. This will give you control and usually more information will then come.

8. Usually past life scenes will have their own conclusion and you will know when it is time to move on. If it seems too long, you may ask what else you need to know about it and then when that is completed, you can stretch well and bring yourself out of it.

9. If you feel heavy after completing the trip, movement such as walking around or stretching can help. Also, writing down what you can remember helps in the release. Drinking some water also helps.

Leading Regressions

If you are leading a regression the following tips may be helpful:

1. Keep your mind on the regression as unrelated thoughts or vibrations from you may confuse the person.

2. When a person is fully in the past life, his or her voice will be very soft. If he or she cries, it will be quite different from normal crying and will seem from long ago.

3. Periodically ask what they are sensing or doing. This helps keep movement going.

4. If the person starts to lose the scene before it's done, guide her back through getting in touch with the body of the past.

5. Keep a calm voice regardless of what the person is experiencing.

6. Do not touch a person who is in regression unless you tell him first, and then only on the upper arm. Touching other areas is too intrusive. Sometimes if a person is having a very difficult time a light touch on the upper arm is helpful. Usually, though, it's distracting.

Let's Go

1. Begin by lying down, with no pillow. Stretch to get the body more relaxed.

2. Develop a dual awareness, so you can be aware of the past life and present life simultaneously.

Do this by:

a. Feeling very heavy and sinking into the floor or bed.

b. Let go of the heaviness and feel light, as though you are floating.

c. Repeat "a."

d. Repeat "b."

e. Feel heavy and light at the same time. This creates a dual awareness.

3. Have the feeling of going backward in time. One of the following visualizations may help you:

a. You may imagine calendar pages going back onto the calendar.

b. The sun going in reverse.

c. Go down a long hallway back into time and open any door that appeals to you.

d. Imagine you are in a time machine going into the past.

4. Use the visualization or focus you have chosen (see page 99). Let your mind ramble so that life can appear or be sensed by you.

5. Watch it for a while. However, if you seem to be only watching and not feeling, put yourself in the body from the past life.

6. After you feel more secure in it you may ask some of the questions listed under #9 in the "Preparing for a Regression" section.

7. Write down your answers, speak into a recorder or, if someone is leading you, perhaps that person will take notes for you.

8. When you have finished, thank the life, stretch well and bring yourself back fully to this life.

Practice makes this easier and a person usually becomes more proficient in time.

It is important to experience past lives if for no other reason than to appreciate the present one more. The veils between past, present, and future are becoming thinner as one's awareness increases. With this more expanded view of life, our growth should accelerate and be easier.

Desire Effects

There are events or opportunities from past lives, present and even future, waiting in a person's force field until a situation and energies are conducive to its manifestation. They are energy forms. When it's almost time for manifestation of one of these forms, the person feels restless as though there were some great void in the self or one's life that is waiting to be filled. It can also feel like a lump of energy waiting to be released or assimilated. They can relate to physical, emotional, mental, or spiritual levels. Primarily, they can relate to personal areas, relationships, careers, or any other facets of life. Sometimes these "new" or "extra" desire effects push themselves in, sometimes they hang around and have an almost negative effect because the person is blocking. The desire effect is on the edge of one's life, waiting to be invited in, expressed, transmuted, or healed. Sometimes it is negative karma to work on. Sometimes it is positive opportunities.

No matter where it is from or where it is headed, it always brings some kind of opportunity with it. When you sense the presence of one of these desire effects around you, pinpoint where in your force field it is located. Then with your mental power think it into your system so you can be aware of its content.

When you feel it in your system, let your mind ramble, let your shoulders be relaxed and see what possibilities come to your awareness. It will help if you expand your consciousness or awareness into it as well. In other words, go to meet it as well as welcoming it in. There is then a better balance of the energy between you and the desire effect.

When you begin to sense the information, let it unfold. Don't try to form it into your preconceived ideas. You will block it. Keep expanding into it.

You may wish to write the information down so you remember it better. Usually it tells of things that will be happening at a later date, although you may realize they are actually in process now.

When you have the information, usually you will have a sense of fulfillment and peace. If not, fill yourself with a lavender color, which heals or erases negative things.

Chapter VIII

DEATH AND AFTER LIFE

DEATH IS NOT PARTICULARLY FASHIONABLE or well thought of. It is rejected by many, ignored by others. Some are even ashamed of dying. They consider it an imperfection. However, it is something that we all must do.

Some people want to live a long time as though that is a great achievement, and one to be valued. Certainly it is—however, the quality of life and growth attained for one's total being are more important.

The most important way to look at death is as part of the cycle of descending into matter—earth, and then ascending into pure spirit—heaven worlds and doing this over and over until we have attained our full development and become at home or at one with the God forces.

Attitudes or Feelings about Death

Not all people, however, have a good grasp of death as being a rebirth into the heaven worlds and have a more earthly attitude towards it. Those people who have a bigger picture of the process can look forward to their deaths more readily. The following are some of the ways different people would like their moment of death to be:

1. As a way to get even with those people who have been neglectful or unloving.

2. Peacefully in sleep, with no foreknowledge of the transition.

3. While having fun, including sex.

4. While working.

5. Peacefully and by themselves so as not to miss any of it.

6. With their spirit walking away from their body. (In this case, the body dies after the spirit has left.)

7. With loved ones around.

8. With prayers of others for a safe, easy transition.

9. With work done.

10. With things in order.

11. In glory—during battle, or while helping others (death being worthwhile if dying for something).

12. Unafraid; feeling confident about going to a new way of being.

13. Not wanting to give up control.

14. Want to have passed on knowledge to descendants, students or someone.

15. Gracefully or dramatically.

16. As Cleopatra did—by retaining beauty. Some would rather die young at the height of their beauty, fame, or fortune rather than to risk old age, being out of power, or being forgotten by others.

17. Die of illness as a way of checking out. He or she wouldn't feel guilty about leaving, then.

Choice Points

Each life we have a certain amount of growth to achieve in terms of our evolution and a certain amount of karma to balance. When a person has completed both, she may be at a choice point where she can die with the goals completed or she can choose to stay on longer, but will have to set new career or personal goals. It will also be necessary to choose certain imbalances or karmic forces on which to focus in the future.

The same person would also have to have a much more expanded view of possibilities because the mere repetition of what she was doing doesn't justify the extra life force involved. When a person has completed the assigned or planned karma and growth and chooses the new goals to work with, the person usually accomplishes a quantum leap in her evolution.

Suicide

There is much difference of opinion and some confusion regarding suicide. Generally, if a person commits suicide, the remainder of his assigned earthly life is lived out in the astral level. It is much more difficult, then, if earthly life were continued. Also, any uncompleted karma or goals would have to be picked up and dealt with in another life.

St. Augustine thought if life were too difficult to handle, it would be all right to go and pick it up another time. There are probably situations where that would be positive. However, generally speaking, it is best to deal with what you have so it doesn't build up and really clobber you in another life.

Some people commit a slow suicide by their tension-producing lifestyles: smoking, drinking, or by other "hazardous to your health" routines.

On occasion it seems all right that a particular person ends his or her own incarnation. Energies surrounding and following the act seem to be destined to happen. Usually, however, the person has made much karma to deal with in terms of respecting life, one's own body, being more careful of how they treat others' feelings, and in fulfilling destiny projects when due. By "when due" we mean at the time it was originally destined so that the project or fulfilled purpose would interface with other destined events. It's like getting the potato salad to the picnic in time to eat and not when everyone is getting ready to leave—only the destined projects or fulfilled purposes are on a much larger scale!

Preparing for Death

Preparing for death should be done at an early age so a person can more fully enjoy life and get the most from it.

Financial preparations are made by many for old age, even funeral expenses are covered. However, for most, a good look at life and death are at best ignored.

How do you feel about death?

1. Can you embrace death as joyfully and enthusiastically as life?

2. Can you see them as part of the same process?

3. What virtues have you most used and developed?

4. What virtues would you yet like to work on in this life?

5. Have you planned some things to accomplish in this life?

6. The fast pace we live in now is forcing us to experience more of the eternal energy. Are you willing to develop beyond the human aspect?

7. Have you developed a philosophy of death and afterlife? Do you know what you are getting into? Or are you fearful of afterlife?

8. Have you gotten in touch with how much your subconscious is planning your death? Do you want to change it?

9. If you hang around until 120 years or more, what kinds of careers would you like to explore?

10. If there truly is a book in each person, what would yours be about and would you like to write it?

11. Is your dream of life big enough?

12. Have you learned to deal with guilt and responsibility so that it doesn't drag you down?

13. Are you caring for your body? Your body is God's gift to you. The shape it is in when you die is your gift back to God.

14. Are you open to changes or "little deaths" in life or are you a control freak?

15. Do you have a philosophy of life to live by?

16. Some people "die" or give up long before their bodies die. They just sort of hang around. Are you willing to really live your life until your lease runs out?

Dying Gracefully

Living life as though you are ready to go anytime and as though you have 100 more years left is a good approach. It may expand your consciousness a bit to be open to both directions at once. However, it will give you a more expanded view of yourself and, hopefully, remove some pressure.

When the moment of death comes, if you are conscious at the time, be aware of your spirit. Let it be lifted and light and open to the death process and to continued life after leaving the body.

Many people who die in fear or pain take that with them into some future life to be worked out. Drowning, death by fire, murder, or starvation are examples of this. It's pretty difficult to open to spirit when you are in great pain or fear.

When a person is about to die there is an energy of transformation that enters the body ahead of time. Sometimes days, weeks, or even a year ahead of time, this process begins. It makes some people very crabby or irritable, others touch base with old friends and family, others feel a need to prepare for this event. Some are not aware that death is what they are preparing for, but the urgency is there anyway.

After Death

Various things happen immediately after death. One fairly common event is when the person who has died appears to someone to let them know he has died. Sometimes people appear to others who previously did not know about the death and also to let them know they still live!

Sometimes a person will seek out living friends or relatives for various reasons only to have them regard her as a ghost. They don't feel very welcome then.

Freedom from pain or bodily limitations, such as retardation or mental problems, will be one of the first experiences. Quite often a sense of bliss and peace fills the person.

Many people have reported seeing a tunnel with light at the other end during the death experience.

Sometimes there are angels, guides, relatives, or friends waiting in the light for them. Much of what a person sees or experiences depends on his or her belief system and spiritual development. People who have not developed much spiritual awareness will find themselves in a grayness or sense of a void.

Whatever total development a person has determines how quickly they go through the stages listed below. If a person is highly developed spiritually but not emotionally, they will be stuck in the emotional review for quite a while. If a person has not developed mentally, that, too, could slow down the process.

There are many versions of what happens to a person after the death of the body. Some say there is a hell. Many people, including the authors, do not believe in a hell of everlasting fire but rather that through our own feelings and attitudes we create heavens or hells in our own systems. If a person has lived a very self-centered life and never learned to be with others he may go into a lower astral plane after death because that is where their vibrations were while they were alive. Without the physical body to modify their energy they will feel the energy more intensely. The hell created when living will intensify. For some people there will be much loneliness, or the sense of being a lost person or lost soul will exist. There is actually a vibration that can fill a person with the feeling of being totally alone or lost and many people find themselves in that vibration after death if that is how they lived on earth. If they had evil feelings they will be immersed into that vibration very heavily when they first die. They may stay there for long periods of time until they begin to long for a better way of being. It is as though they have created a shell or cocoon with these negative energies that block out all else.

If a person lives a loving life and one filled with interest in growth, then life after death will be wonderful. The heaven the person created while she was living will be intensified after death.

Life between Lives

The only thing we lose of ourselves when we die is our physical bodies. Our thoughts, emotions, attitudes, memories, and attachments all remain with us as we cross over to the other side. Jealousies, hates, loves, desires—none of these die with the physical body. If you are addicted to alcohol or drugs—the addiction goes right along with you. If you are a searcher for knowledge or for wisdom in the physical body you will take those tendencies with you also. Only when a person tires of the way he is and wants to change is he free to make a change, to learn and develop. This is true whether in the physical body or free of it. The Guides, Helpers, Teachers, whatever name you wish to give those highly evolved beings who work as messengers of God, are always willing to help anyone who wants to learn but they will not take responsibility for anyone's decision to change.

Sometimes a person doesn't realize for quite a while that he is dead. This person is said to be "earthbound" and will hang around familiar places and friends and try to get them to hear him. It is very frustrating when they do not. After a while, the person may hear someone talk about his death, or may see something that helps bring the realization of what has happened. There are people who work with those who have just "crossed over," to help them understand what has happened and what they can do now. There are people who are trained or gifted in this work, and there are also those on the other side whose job is to do this type of work as well. Most living people work and study at night in their higher bodies, while the physical body is asleep, and some of these people could be helping with this type of work also during sleep. There are always many who are ready to help the newly departed accept and understand the new surroundings, duties, and growth opportunities.

Sometimes the person is in a state of shock and may be in a "sleeping" type of situation for a while. If the person has had an extremely trying and confusing life or had to endure prolonged periods of extreme pain before crossing over, this sleeping or resting period can last many years. Usually, though, this condition does not last very long.

Sometimes a person finds herself in a beautiful nature area. There may be a lake, gardens, beautiful meadows or scenes. This also helps a person rest while adjusting to the new way of "life."

There is a grayness where some people spend time, and some people think this is what the Catholics call "purgatory." Many feel this is only a brief period of confusion and adjusting to the fact that there is no longer a physical vehicle and that time spent there need be only very brief if the person will begin looking for the "spiritual light" and growth. The faith or belief of the individual in never ceasing continuation of life would have quite a strong bearing here.

Thought-power there is very strong and, by focused thinking, a person can find or choose where they want to visit. Some people do this here, of course, by the method we know as astral traveling.

This time between lives can, and should, be used to review what you've done in the life just previous and what you want to accomplish in the next life. Some rush back into another life without this reviewing period. Many indications are that we have free will in this area. We can be reborn as God's plan would naturally carry us along or we may make our own choice.

Those who have evolved further will spend more of their time, in most cases, between lives devoting themselves to helping and guiding others. They might help guide people living in physical bodies, they may choose to work with those on the other side, or both. This is where the term "spirit guides" comes from. To be a true guide, the guide should be more highly evolved than the ones they are helping. Otherwise, only spiritual contact would be involved, but not true guidance. However, it can be true that less evolved souls will work as apprentices under the direction of the higher guides.

Etheric Level

The etheric level is a higher form of the physical body and relates to the etheric plane or level. This is the first area that a person goes through upon death. Some pass right through while others may remain there for years. They are sometimes called lost souls. It is a colorless void, sometimes called a "grayness," empty of everything, for some. For others, they still see their earthly haunts, only in the grim grayness and may not realize they are dead for a while. These are the earth-bound souls. Others may remain in it for quite a while because they don't realize where they are or what they are to be doing.

Some will immediately begin their work for this area—that of recollection and preparing for the next steps. This is a time to take inventory of what your needs are for growth and what you want to accomplish in your development. It is not necessary for some to stay in this plane because they have already been working on this and are aware of what they need or want to study next. In one example, a scientist did not use his knowledge wisely and spent several earth years in this area because of his own choice. He felt he need-ed this time to see how he had not lived up to what he was capable of and what he felt he needed to do for his own spiritual development. After his time spent on the Astral and Mental Planes, he returned to earth in a situation of his own choosing—that of a very simple life with none of the material advantages he had in his previous life. He had all of the material advantages in his previous life and wanted none of them in the next.

One gentleman who was regressed to a time when he was in this void just after his death described his feelings this way, "Feeling of helplessness, felt sus-pended above the ground, in a gray fog, unable to contact the ground or anything around me. Couldn't move except for my eyes. The feeling of being helpless and unwanted was very strong. The feeling of being unable to do anything to help myself was very depressing ... nothing but gray fog." This followed a life in which he had died of the flu, alone in a rooming house, with no friends or family. The life itself had been a rather gray one and he had chosen to not have much contact with other people. The loneliness followed him to his current life.

Astral Level

One of the functions of the astral plane is that of extrasensory perception. It is the plane reached by many people through astral projection and is the source of much psychic phenomena. But one of the most important functions of this plane is that of a "gymnasium," a place to work out problems. This is one of the areas we go to in our dreams to work out things we do not want to face when we are awake or when we need better understanding. It is also the plane to clean ourselves out emotionally as much as possible before going onto the next plane. Again, there are people who do not need to spend much time here, others will spend quite awhile, depending on their development and desire to learn.

For an example of how you can work on your problems on this plane, think of some of your own dreams. What monsters have you had to face in your dreams? What parts of yourself have you seen clothed in the body of someone else with those traits good or bad because you couldn't face them in yourself? How many times have you apologized to a friend or enemy in a dream when you couldn't face them when you were awake? Desires are expressed here as well.

Mental Level

This has a variety of functions. To gain comprehension of how you have done so far and what you want to do are a part of the work on this plane. As on the other planes so far mentioned a person can conjure up images of whatever he wishes to see by his thought power. By your thought power, you can see what you wish. If it is conducive to your learning to be surrounded by hills or mountains, that is what you will see. If you would prefer to see a metropolis, you may see that. We still carry moods with us to this plane and are allowed to see what can help us to learn better. All self-progressing is done from this plane or the planes below. Some of the self-progressing is done by helping others.

A description of the learning process on this plane was given in a regression by a young man as follows: "I could wander around in class or go away. When I came back it was as though I hadn't missed anything. I started in where I had left off. No two people received the same thing or in the same way. Each person learned at his or her own level. The Soul (who was teaching) wasn't talking but when you were there you received what you needed (as though absorbed individually). He was soft white, just basically aglow. His form wasn't very large. Size doesn't count there—brightness counts. I was taught to listen for vibrations and feelings from everything. I was taught not to have bitterness, especially for my death (killed in battle in Italy, World War II), taught patience, understanding, love of creatures or anything connected with nature and to accept what cannot be changed."

Intuitional/Compassionate Level

There are no moods here—no seeking for understanding. The soul is filled with understanding. This is an attunement with the rest of the Universe and with God. Usually people spend only a brief period of time here; there is very little problem in continuing to the next plane. As with all of the planes, people in their physical lives can reach this area through meditation or other means, for varying lengths of time.

Will/Spirit Level

People with strong egos sometimes can get stuck here. A person's will may be very powerful. This is the level of blending one's will with Divine will in order to progress.

Many entities who help people still in their earth bodies come from this level and are called guides or helpers. The less positive ones find that they can still exert power and control. The more positive ones are excellent sources of information and strength.

However, if you work with guides or helpers it is best to find some from the soul level or higher as they are into developing your essence. Whatever is best for you helps determine how they work. Many on the will/spirit level, however, are more interested in their own agenda.

Soul Level

This is a special level to attain and only the good that you have done affects this area. It is too high a vibration for negativity to stick. However, if there is an area of self that you haven't developed, the corresponding areas of your own soul level will have a void. This void pulls you back into life to have experiences to fill these voids.

When people reach this level after death they are into the pure essence of soul.

Divine Level or One with God

The "seventh heaven" is a phrase many are familiar with. It is one of great joy and bliss. This Divine Level is a seventh level and certainly is a seventh level in the heaven world. Many people feel that a person always touches this level and has contact with God before reincarnating again.

Those who have achieved the ability to function on this level are truly in the presence of God. They would only reincarnate if another earthly life would be helpful in the overall development of earth.

Reaching these Levels while on Earth

People still in the body may, through meditation, prayers, or other devotional practices, develop abilities to function on these vibratory levels while still in the physical body. The vibrations usually aren't as clear and powerful, however, except in peak experiences.

The above descriptions of the various planes are short and incomplete. There are divisions within each plane that have not been mentioned. There are also higher octaves of these planes.

Why come back to the physical life when there are opportunities to learn and gain understanding on the other side? It is far easier to work things through on the physical plane for our development. We need both the physical lives and the time spent in the other side between lives for our growth in our journey to "one-ness-with-God."

Prayer for Those on the Other Side

The question occasionally comes—"Should we pray for those on the other side?" Yes, if we cared enough for a person's well-being on this side to pray for him or her, why not continue the caring and praying? We all need sincere, loving prayers from others whether we are in the physical body or not. We need all the help we can get! A man, now on the other side, who spent his last life on earth as a Protestant minister, asked us to get in touch with his son and ask that he pray for him. He said he needed his prayers and com-mented, "We Protestants aren't taught to pray for our dead and we need your prayers over here." His son was contacted and did pray for his father and after-wards commented that he felt much better himself since praying for his father.

It's best to give your prayer energy to God to use as God sees fit for the particular person for whom you are praying. What we think would be best for some-one may not be God's idea of best. It helps to keep us from meddling that way, too!

That those on the other side may need our prayers for release from earth after death is evidenced by the experience a professional man had. He had lost his young daughter unexpectedly and couldn't "let go of her." It was affecting his work as well as his emotional well-being. We helped him to make contact with her. In their conversation she asked him for prayers to help her in her release. He, too, gained release and more. In a letter written about a month later, he states, "It has been so good and a real sense of growing between my daughter and me, since your intervention and guidance. I am more and more aware of her at worship—especially Holy Communion and she is now to me a real resource 'over there' enabling me to move on and to grow with her encouragement and 'Come on, Daddy—don't be afraid, it's all right.' It's been such a step forward for me and I know now what was hanging me up and holding her back—so the leavetaking was so great—so real and so releasing to us both, and I shall always recall with love and warmth and deep gratitude your part in it—with my daughter and me."

Chapter IX
REBIRTH AND CHILDREN

WE DO NOT COME INTO THIS WORLD as newborn children among total strangers. Our relatives and friends have been with us in a variety of relationships in our previous lives. Parents are sometimes reborn as children of their former children. Sisters may have been mothers, children, aunts, or friends. Brothers may have been fathers, children, uncles, or friends. We learn to live with, love, and accept others in a variety of relationships under many different circumstances.

Babies may arrive with bag and baggage from past lives, which may make rearing them very difficult or fairly easy. Of course, parents can add their own difficulties to the family situation and really make it interesting! But there is an overall joy in the thought of having an opportunity to help guide another soul in his travels. It is not always easy to see the struggle a child may be going through—to take the time to listen to each child and get to know that person. It is necessary in order to gain understanding of each child's particular problems. The error in thinking each child is a "new" soul with no previous experience, concerns, fears, or poor personality traits can lead to much misunderstanding.

Children do not always think as their parents do. Each person comes into a particular life with their own peculiar thought patterns and ways of reacting. All individuals have their own unique histories and their own unique personalities. These differences show up in children and cause different kinds of behavior. For instance, if one child had been a pirate on the high seas for several lives and another child had always been a quiet person, too shy to really accomplish what he should in his lives, then the parents would be wrong to emphasize the same type of training for one as for the other.

Can you imagine the difficulty that may arise if a child was formerly a parent of one or both of his parents? He may subconsciously be carrying an authoritative attitude toward them and think and act like he knows more than they do.

Also, imagine the difficulty for two parents who have always been generous, self-giving souls having a child born to them with the opposite traits for the purpose of learning how to be *more* generous and self-giving. If the parents expect the child naturally to be like them and not need special help with her growth in that area, they are in for a surprise.

Or what of the gentle, beautiful little girl with very morbid streaks and unreasonable fears? Would it not help the parents to know she had had several violent, traumatic lives just previous to the present one and is learning to live without such fears in this life and learning to control her own emotions? It would be much easier to understand and guide her.

The person who has turned from the spiritual development that he should have may choose to be born into a family where that is emphasized.

People about to enter back into life on earth usually have some say about who he or she will have as parents. If the "wheel of karma," that is, strong karmic energy, is present, the person may not have total say! The person may even not want to be reborn at that time or to those parents.

Some reasons for choosing parents are:

1. Wanting to return to people who are loving and supportive.

2. Looking for parents to help them achieve their goals or work out karma.

3. A person who has lived many lives in lower ways may chose an upstanding set of parents who can guide them into better lifestyles. Sometimes this doesn't take and a really good family will find they have a black sheep among them and wonder why. All that they have done to help the child will some day register, however.

4. The genes they will inherit from the particular parents may help them progress in certain areas.

5. The life the parents have chosen may relate well to what the incoming child wants to be involved in.

6. The incoming child may have been a part of the family already and died young. Sometimes they were born previously to the current grandparents and want to be back with them.

7. Sometimes a person has a child that is very difficult and she seems to be helpless in guiding the child. Never say, "If that were my child I would raise him or her right." You may find in a later life that the particular child is now yours and basically is just plain difficult.

Sometimes an incoming entity will be pushy about his future parents getting together and creating the body for him. There usually are three entities at conception: papa, mama, and future baby.

The incoming entity does not stay with the fetus all the time. It may astral travel and be doing other things. However, the more it stays and helps in the development of the body, the more aware and strong he or she will be after birth. People who talk, sing, or otherwise relate to the unborn child will usually find that their baby is much more "present" and interactive at early stages. They can also want a lot of attention.

Sometimes parents will have a difficult time relating to their new baby. There may be unresolved energies from a past life or the baby may actually not be in a great mood after birth!

If a person dies in an unhappy state such as loneliness, irritability, fearfulness, or under some other unpleasant vibration it may actually activate that energy when they are back in a body. Although we have new bodies, our energies from past lives affect them.

A child suffering from colic may actually be feeling pain from a previous life. For instance, if a person dies of cancer, the etheric residue of the infected area may create pain in the new body. Healing can be very helpful to newborns if there is indication of unpleasant carryovers.

Most of the time, however, the old energies fade and the baby settles into its new body quite well.

Multiple Births

In the case of multiple births, it may be entities wanting to share a closer relationship or it may be that karmically they need to work out problems with one another.

It also may simply be a case of "car-pooling"—two or more entities wanting to be born to the same parents, at the same time.

Early Deaths

Sometimes the baby will find the stress of the new life too difficult or be fearful. If the will to live isn't that strong, the child may die and try again at a later date.

There are instances when an entity needs to go through illness or suffering in order to develop. When the learning is complete, the body may no longer be inhabitable or the entity may choose to go on back to the heaven worlds, thus leaving the body to die.

Sometimes it's a planned thing before parents or children are born. The parents may also learn and grow from the events concerning the baby. If the death wasn't destined, the child will sometimes live out its specified days on the astral plane, learning and growing there.

It is very hard to lose a child. It may help if a person can focus more on the entity or person the child was and know that they have been with that person before and will be again.

Some babies or children seem so frustrated being in the small body that they haven't fully learned to use yet. Babies especially have memories of their most recent past. They are very aware, however, they can't operate the body enough to share things. People trained to talk psychically to babies sometimes get some rather interesting information. Sometimes parents will sense the thoughts of the child, also.

Developing Identity

Children sometimes share memories of past lives—usually in short statements—such as, "I used to be a teacher," or "I was killed in a car accident." It's as though they aren't aware of what it really means. It's just a fleeting memory.

On occasion it will be more than a fleeting memory and the child may be fearful. For instance, one child was afraid of cumulus clouds, thinking the clouds might hurt her. In checking her past life it was found that she had been injured and later died in the atomic bomb at Nagasaki (large cloud).

Another example was of a little boy who was afraid to have others touch him. His body was fearful because he was tortured in a previous life.

Usually as the children get more fully into the new body and new life, the painful memories go away. Sometimes praying for healing of memories and pain can help.

There is a very positive use of these early memories and that is to bring creative abilities through. Artistic things should be taught and encouraged in children. This helps bring these talents into today's consciousness and it also helps to develop a more unified right and left brain function. Creativity is one of the greatest ways for a child (or an adult) to develop his or her own identity.

Memory Books

Scrapbooks that contain photos and captions along with stories of events in the child's life can help them in establishing a clearer identity. They can be called "Remember When" books, allowing the child to review what he or she has done or where they've been.

International Awareness

Children who are taught about other cultures early, before they learn to be prejudiced, will have an easier time adjusting to the greater world. Children need to be given more than a local consciousness. Their memories of other cultures may also be triggered, helping them to understand more.

Spirituality

Most children have a natural openness to God, Christ, angels, and other spiritual beings. Teaching them general concepts about eternal life—always living—and that they may change bodies and have different lives, can give them a better foundation for facing death. This includes understanding the death of pets, relatives, or friends. It can help alleviate fears of their own deaths.

Since knowledge of God and other spiritual beings is usually easily grasped by a child, it can help also in developing a sense of themselves and life in general. It can be helpful and sometimes surprising to the adult to ask what the child thinks of God, other spiritual beings, and heaven.

Unfolding of a Person

Although a child comes to this life with lots of baggage, talents, hopes, and drives, she will still need to unfold as the new person. Encouraging a child to share her inner self is a blessing in helping her unfold. This can be encouraged by listening and conversing with the child. A child, when listened to, learns to express herself. Communication skills develop through sharing.

One of the greatest gifts you can give a child or adult is to recognize her as an individual worth getting to know. Love is not enough. Personal recognition and inspiration to unfold the self are very important.

Chapter X

DEVELOPMENT

SOMETIMES IT IS DIFFICULT TO RECOGNIZE if we are achieving the growth we would like. This chapter includes information and exercises that can benefit.

Soul Level Development

A chakra is located in the upper chest (see Heart Chakra, Figure 3, page 53) that relates to love, compassion, and our ability to achieve soul level development. The energy in this soul level chart is divided into twelve sections (see Chart 2, page 135).

The good that we have developed from our past lives, genetic energy, astrological and numerological energy, as well as other positive things we learn from other sources, goes to our soul level to fill in the voids. The soul then becomes a fully developed entity, or unit of consciousness. Any negativity in your life does not affect the soul, because the soul is in such a high vibration so that only the higher level of achievements, awarenesses, and understandings can reach it. What negative things can do is separate the personality from the soul and thus slow down growth. The negativity can also perpetuate the voids in the soul causing the person to repeat patterns over and over until finally the person achieves the learning.

The exercise we are about to do is based on what you have achieved for your soul, not just this life, but others as well. You may see past life situations and recognize you are still working on some of these same things. You may be aware of things you are beginning.

In previous lives accelerated evolution wasn't as strong as it is now. Therefore, development of this area becomes more important.

1. *Divine Love.* The unconditional, all-encompassing love. Go deeply into it. Feel it.

   How well are you doing with this in this life?

   Is there something from this or a past life that is hindering further development?

2. *Joy and Acceptance.* This is a beautiful, joyful acceptance of life with contentment wherever you are. It brings a willingness to really live whether in or out of a body.

   How well are you doing with this in this life?

   Is there something from this or a past life that is hindering further development?

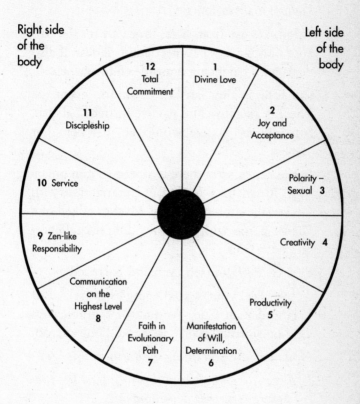

Right side
of the
body

Left side
of the
body

12
Total
Commitment

1
Divine Love

11
Discipleship

2
Joy and
Acceptance

10 Service

Polarity –
Sexual 3

9 Zen-like
Responsibility

Creativity 4

Communication
on the
Highest Level
8

Productivity
5

Faith in
Evolutionary
Path
7

Manifestation
of Will,
Determination
6

Chart 2. Soul Level Energy

3. *Polarity–Sexual.* It is a higher form of polarity. Sex is but a part of its manifestation in our lives. Other areas include opposites: in or out; heat or cold; heaven or earth; human or Divine; male or female.

Paradoxes are from here. It deals with the balance of opposites or a need for evenness. It also deals with balancing opposites into oneness.

Samadhi is the Sanskrit term for evenness. There is an active and passive form of balance. Samadhi as passive would be just being or "isness."

In the active form there is a need to join polarities. It can be a feeling of polarization with God or the supreme energy. Mystics talked of a Divine union with God, blending sexual energies with God.

Passive: Feel yourself even and balanced.

Active: Feel your sexual energies polarized or balanced with God. We talk of a union with God on spiritual levels, we should on sex, too.

How well are you doing with this in this life?

Is there something from this or a past life that is hindering further development?

4. *Creativity.* God-like creativity. This is the ability to see deeply into life, recognize creativity and help create it. It is more than drawing tulips and buttercups, although if this energy comes in, make it a holy activity. This creative

energy can be used in all of life—relationships, career, etc.

How well are you doing with this in this life?

Is there something from this or a past life that is hindering further development?

5. *Productivity.* This is an action branch of God. We are the arms and legs so that the God-force can work through us. How willing are you to be open to that? The mundane can be Divine.

How well are you doing with this in this life?

Is there something from this or a past life that is hindering further development?

6. *Manifestation of Will, Determination.* This area involves staying with what you are doing, or fighting for what you feel is right. You may find you are going until second and third winds come through. This involves going beyond ordinary capabilities. The manifestation part includes mentally and spiritually causing things to happen.

How well are you doing with this in this life?

Is there something from this or a past life that is hindering further development?

(Note: The first six have much to do with one's own growth and development. The remaining six have to do with work in the world or universe. Stretch well before beginning and then stretch again after the first three.)

7. *Faith in Evolutionary Path.* This is the process of growth—becoming your own path and helping others to become their own paths and recognizing the greater purposes of growth and evolution. All things work together for those who love God.

How well are you doing with this in this life?

Is there something from this or a past life that is hindering further development?

8. **Communication on the Highest Level.** Being aware of all. Knowing how things got the way they are and where they are going. You can feel the pain and suffering of the world without being caught up in it. It brings an understanding of why some people need heavy experiences in order to grow. You can be caring and helpful, but not caught up in it.

How well are you doing with this in this life?

Is there something from this or a past life that is hindering further development?

9. *A Zen-like Responsibility.* You do what there is to do while being in total accord with your evolutionary path in terms of working with it. You teach because things are there to teach. You smile because people are there to be smiled at. You allow energies to move through you.

How well are you doing with this in this life?

Is there something from this or a past life that is hindering further development?

10. *Service.* This is similar to #9 in terms of responsibility but has a deeper quality. This is Master status. Masters serve. Healing flows through, enlightenment flows through, doing for others, being for others. This is a higher form of being a channel.

    How well are you doing with this in this life?

    Is there something from this or a past life that is hindering further development?

    (Note: Sometimes people want God to do things for them but don't want to be a part of doing things for others.)

11. *Discipleship.* This includes spending time with God. Learning is a part of this. It includes the deepest secrets, how mystical energy works, what is beyond evolution. You carry out Divine wishes from this area.

    How well are you doing with this in this life?

    Is there something from this or a past life that is hindering further development?

12. *Total Commitment.* This is a true oneness with God. You are no longer a disciple, but as Christ said, "I and the Father are One." You are functioning from the God level—total attunement, awareness, love, etc. It is the culmination of the growth path.

    How well are you doing with this in this life?

    Is there something from this or a past life that is hindering further development?

This exercise is difficult. However, it does open you up to greater growth, even if you don't get much the first time you do it.

Growth

Since growth or development is our main reason for being on earth, it should be a primary focus for all ages of life. Sometimes people get caught up in productivity or enjoyment of life, thus getting their priorities out of focus.

Believing in and connecting with one's creator—God, or whatever name you choose to give that energy, is the first step in any healthy growth. It gives us an overall focus or goal, the sense of returning to our beginnings as a completion of our journeys.

Life is our main teacher. Before we are born we "set up" our desired goals for this life. We have a plan of action or blueprint for the coming life. However, once we are in the body it may be difficult to remember what was previously decided. It's as though we lost our instruction books!

However, all things that we learn will help us even though we may not feel we are exactly where we'd like to be. Chapter XII has information that can help in understanding some of the growth experiences.

Where's the Teacher?

It is often said that when the student is ready, the teacher arrives. It is not always as we think, however. Sometimes the teacher may be a life situation to work through, or it may be a book, or the teaching may come through your own meditations and insights.

Some people desperate for spiritual growth teachings may find themselves isolated from such information. This is usually a sign that the person needs to learn from expanding awareness and comprehension of what's in and around him. Prayer and meditation as well as practicing focused awareness can help.

—Exercise—
Focused Awareness

Each day choose something to focus on. At first choose something very easy. It may be:

✦ *Listening to birds singing.*

✦ *Looking for and observing a certain kind or color of flower.*

✦ *Watching how many times you complain about something.*

✦ *Watching how many times you are happy over something.*

✦ *Feeling wind on your face.*

✦ *Light and shadow patterns created by the sun.*

It should be something simple to begin with so that it can be more fun and more easily accomplished.

Later you may wish to choose one area or facet of life in which to immerse yourself. This practice is similar to forming a wedge into higher dimensions. One of the authors chose a Lenten Season to focus on St. Paul and totally be immersed in his explanation of Christ and Christ's message, as well as the essence of

St. Paul himself. The results were staggering, with visions appearing as well as insights in many areas. Direct voice contact with guides was also achieved which continued and developed. There was further understanding of how St. Paul was trying to help a new movement—Christianity—from getting so far out that it turned others away. Some Christians think he may have held back too much, however!

The area of study or focus can be as simple as growing iris or some other plants or trees. It can be more complex, like learning about some concept that is new to you. When a person does this it brings a deeper wisdom.

—Meditation—
Finding Your Focus

Write down all the things you think you might like to do, no matter how silly or ambitious. After writing them down, go back over them. Which ones stand out or really catch your attention? Give it some serious thought. You may wish to begin by choosing something that doesn't cost too much or take too much time. Give yourself the freedom to quit if it doesn't seem to be what you want. Then choose something else.

Teachers and Gurus

All of us teach one another at some point in life, sometimes not so pleasantly, either. But for many there comes a time in life when it seems imperative to intensify learning and to find outside help. Teachers or gurus may be sought.

Finding a teacher or guru whose teachings most relate to your philosophies is a good place to begin. In this Aquarian Age, we need to have a variety of people to learn from. Many people are finding that they are their own paths and, although they need guidance and directions at times, the urge to turn one's life over to someone else is just not there.

Others have turned their lives over to gurus or teachers and made great growth, later finding that it is not enough for them.

It is best to become involved in learning that leads you to develop answers from inside yourself.

Teachers and Students Reincarnating Together

Many times teachers and students will continue that relationship in future lives. The teacher develops more and the student is able to learn more.

Sometimes teachers and students change roles in various lives. This can enrich understanding. Sometimes it leads to a situation where the persons not only learn from one another, but they may work together in leading others.

There are many variations of the teacher/student relationship, but nowhere is it stronger than in the self. We are our own teacher and student.

—Meditation—
Teacher/Student

Be in a meditative state.
    a. What are you trying to teach yourself?
    b. What are you trying to learn from yourself?

Kundalini and Reincarnation

The Kundalini or Evolutionary energy is very much a part of reincarnation. Depending on one's evolution and the genetic development of your parents, you will have a certain amount of Kundalini already available at birth. The amount and usability will give you your intelligence.

If you have a great deal available and usable, you will be more at genius level. If the energy isn't readily usable, as in the case of an underdeveloped ego or a body with poor or little cell refinement, mental, emotional, and physical problems may result. Problems with mental illness may also result.

Usually the Kundalini energy will work on the refinement and development of the system by itself.

People with underdeveloped egos will have a tendency to put themselves down and block growth, including development of the Kundalini energy or the person may have an over-inflated ego to compensate for the lack of development. A healthy ego is very important in one's growth.

Kundalini and Prana

When a person has excessive or unusable Kundalini, getting enough prana (a life force) can help. Prana comes through the breath and also through the cells of the body. Our main source is the sun. Many people find themselves drawn to the sun in order to help fill the body's needs. If a person gets too much of the sun's prana there is a tendency to feel intoxicated or heavy. People who naturally absorb all they need will find being in the sun difficult and that they feel excessively heavy. These people will like cloudy days and evenings or night more than a sunny day.

Kundalini, Enlightenment, and Gifts

When portions of the Kundalini energy are completely developed and usable it will turn into enlightenment or gifts. Enlightenment includes wisdom and intuitive abilities. Gifts include superhuman strength, awareness, and healing.

For further information on enlightenment and gifts, as well as Kundalini, please refer to *Kundalini and the Chakras* by Genevieve Lewis Paulson.

Developing Kundalini Each Life

Although a person may achieve high use of the Kundalini during a lifetime, it will need to be developed and "tamed" again in succeeding lives. However, it is usually easier each time a person really works with it.

Finding Your Direction—Karmic Drive

One of the strongest forces affecting our lives is that of karmic drive, which consists of strong desires or expectations for past lives. They may be your own or they may be others' expectations for you. The unfulfilled desires or expectations become karmic in nature in that they are looking for fulfillment.

They can affect all areas of life. However, one of the most predominant has to do with one's place in the world, community, family, or career. Where do we fit in, or do we need to carve out our own place?

—Meditation—
Karmic Drive

Be in a meditative state. Tune into your solar plexus. When you feel a strong connection with the energies there, ask the solar plexus consciousness the following.

What is my karmic drive in relationship to:
- ✦ *Career*
- ✦ *Family*
- ✦ *Other relationships*
- ✦ *Community*
- ✦ *World*

If you don't get answers for some of the areas you may have worked them out, not had any, or it may not be time to see them. The exercise may be repeated some other time only to find you have new things on your agenda.

If you do not like what comes through, bless it and ask it to change to something easier or better.

Visions and Intuitions

Sometimes we will have visions or intuitions of things we could achieve, but it doesn't seem to be happening. It may be for any of the following reasons:

1. You may have heard or seen the information while in expanded consciousness. In this case, it usually cannot happen until you can spend longer times in that expanded consciousness so it can manifest. There are many possibilities waiting for us when our consciousness expands and develops enough to do them.

2. You may be seeing something that is destined to happen years later.

3. Check over your interpretation of the vision or intuition. It may be manifesting in a different manner from what you first perceived.

4. You may have talked too much about the vision or intuition and blown its energy, so it couldn't manifest.

5. You may be blocking its manifestation through fear, disbelief, or not wanting to work hard enough for it to happen. Many times people don't want to expend the effort it takes to accomplish something.

—Meditation—
Opening to an Intuition

Let yourself see the vision or feel the intuition again. Don't try to change it. Just go for the original input. Sit with its energy, let it expand. What other information comes to you?

Expanding Consciousness

When we live from a limited consciousness, our knowledge and possibilities are limited. We may feel trapped, in a rut, bored or directionless. The following is an exercise that may help.

—Meditation—
Gathering Information

Be in a meditative state.
  a. Expand the energy out around your head, especially the top. Be aware of it. Also be

> *aware of energy in your heart and solar plexus.*
>
> b. *Ask what else there is for you to know. Just let your mind ramble for a while. Don't reject anything during this period.*
>
> c. *Write down the information you received or felt. Then you may make choices from what you received.*

We can only work with what we can perceive. Reading and talking with others are other ways to expand perceptions and thus open up to new possibilities.

Rigid Philosophies

If a person becomes rigid in his or her own philosophy, never being open to other opinions or ideas, growth will be blocked.

It isn't a matter of finding the "right" truth and staying with it. It's a process of finding new and greater truths for more expanded levels of comprehension.

—Meditation—
Expanding Truths

Be in a meditative state.
>
> a. *What belief systems hold you back?*
>
> b. *What new level of truth wants to be recognized?*

Inner and Outer Truths

Many people hold certain beliefs to themselves as a part of their inner truth. However, they express totally different views as a part of their outer truths. Sometimes these truths are completely opposite. This can cause strain and tension over the years and one day the truth needs to be reconciled.

—Meditation—
Inner and Outer Truths

Be in a meditative state.
> *a. What inner and outer truths do you have that are completely opposite?*
>
> *b. What inner and outer truths are you bringing closer together?*

Awakened but not Fully Enlightened

Many people have reached an awakened state in which they recognize other states of consciousness or being, have a greater awareness of other realities, such as reincarnation. However, they don't understand these energies enough to make greater or full use of them. The following are some steps a person can take to help facilitate greater enlightenment.

1. Be aware as much as possible of what is going on around you and in you. How can you use this new information?

2. Open to spiritual consciousness several times a day—prayer and meditation are excellent.

3. Open to contact with your Creator—the supreme energy (God). Develop a closer relationship to your source.

4. Watch your yearnings and desires. Do they enhance or impede your growth?

5. Include service to others as a part of your life. This helps open miracle energy for all.

6. Practice oneness—with God, others, nature, and yourself.

7. Develop your brain system—that is the main way we compute greater enlightenment.

8. Develop your feelings and sense as further ways of comprehending enlightenment.

9. Open to rhythm in yourself—the whole universe has rhythm.

Chapter XI
TESTS AND STEPS ALONG THE PATH

WHEN PEOPLE CONNECT MORE FULLY with their high mental and spiritual aspects, strange things begin to happen. Some people consider these events and feelings as tests, whereas others see them as steps along the path. It doesn't really matter what you call them. However, if you call them steps you may find it a little easier. The purpose of these steps is threefold:

1. To develop a mystical closeness with your source.

2. To be able to handle and use very strong frequencies of energies that will transpose you into a greater being.

3. To be so in tune with evolution and cosmic purpose that you see and appreciate the wisdom of the path you are given. Poverty or

riches, happiness or suffering, being or doing,
fullness or emptiness, recognition by others or
just another face in the crowd would be the
vehicles that would only serve to help you
achieve your purpose. Your joys and completeness would come through your willingness to serve.

People who are destined to become teachers, work
with others on their paths, or help make major
changes in the world usually go through these events
more frequently and with greater intensity.

We develop in all areas, physically, emotionally,
mentally and spiritually. Sometimes a person will
make great progress on one level and not the others. If
you develop too far on one level and neglect the others, the neglected levels will pull you back. This is so
that you can work with them in a more synchronized
fashion. When one area is developed out of proportion, your life may be lopsided and you may find your
growth not as effective or pleasant as it might be. You
can help this process of growth by meditating regular-
ly and including some attention for all of these areas.
The following tests and steps are not listed in chronological order because there is no chronological order.
This is because each person develops differently.

Going Off-Center

Sometimes people will feel that they have lost the ability to stay cool, calm, and collected. They will find
themselves deeply involved emotionally or mentally.
Their energies will seemingly be out of control. If you
find this happening to you, don't hassle yourself and

don't try to block the excessive energies or the excessive moods. Go into it—what is it teaching you?

Also, what experience is opening to you? We learn best by experience and need to give ourselves the freedom. Freedom to feel the pain, freedom to experience, freedom to go to the depths, to go to the heights. It takes a lot of strength to do this sometimes because there may be a lot of heavy pain or confusion. People may ask, "what's the matter with me—as evolved as I am I shouldn't be having this. I should know better, I should be able to handle this." However, you find you are pushed beyond the old limits of what you've handled before. You will be forced to let go of ego attachment and really experience. It is as though you are the center or hub of a wheel. You need freedom to be able to go from the center all the way out the spokes to the outer rim, to the outer edges and really feel it and learn from it.

This will expand your horizons and capabilities. You will then reconnect with your center in a new, deeper way. Your faith will be greater and you will be able to experience all of life in a deeper way.

Limbo

Everyone experiences this one many times and in many areas of life. It happens when you move from one level to another in your growth. Old ways of being disappear and the new isn't quite with you yet. When you are in between levels you will feel as though you are in limbo and can't seem to connect anywhere. There is no support from the old way of being and the new level has to be absorbed into you before it becomes usable. This is a difficult time to handle no matter whether the level change is large or small.

Some people let go of jobs or are fired during this phase, or relationships may shift or end. They may find their philosophy and approach to life changing.

One of the best things to do during one of these periods is to clean out clutter. It may be clutter in drawers, on desks or tables, or in your emotions or thoughts. Look at the areas in your life that need cleaning out.

Meditating, exploring, and reading are all ways of opening to the future. Asking in a meditative state what else you need to let go of and what new things want to come in may speed the progress. Also, time is needed for these changes to happen.

Power

Power is not a dirty word. However, it can be misused. The right use of this energy is important because without it you cannot handle and use the higher energies. They may wipe you out instead. As you own your own power and learn to use it well, you will find that you can open to a higher power.

In learning to handle this energy you will find yourself pulled into many different situations that will force you to identify and use this power. Recognizing that you are on the "power" step may help in using it wisely. Sometimes one uses power wisely by holding oneself back from interfering where one shouldn't.

As with all the steps the wisdom of Solomon would certainly help. However, we wouldn't then learn through experience.

Opening to Collective Unconscious

The collective unconscious is the group memory of all the humans, all the races. It's the group subconscious for the planet and it flows through you as well as it flows through everyone else. When you have done a lot of cleaning on yourself you may find you've touched into this area.

On this you may think you're in some real trouble. In Christian terminology you would be under conviction of sin. You're going to think how really bad you are. You may wonder, "What's the matter with me?" You'll feel so down on yourself you can't believe it. What's happening here is that you're cleaning out your connection with the collective unconscious.

Every time you have a negative thought, turn it to something positive. It is as though you are redeeming the negative energies of the world and turning them to positive.

Love Relationships

One of the very difficult steps for a person is to find that he or she is hopelessly and deeply in love with someone, so much so that his or her insides seem to be at the mercy of a Mixmaster. This is not the same as when you are in love, where you may have all the turning, churning feelings inside. This is when you feel yourself being pulled off track by a strong relationship that seemingly goes nowhere. It may be that the other person is married or disinterested or the other person may not feel the same way you do.

One's relationship with God, one's Creator, should be the primary love relationship in a person's life. Any relationship that takes away from that is liable to end because too much energy will have been put into it. One learns also to love without attachment.

Occupation

Many times people will find themselves in occupations, relationships, or situations that do not seem to make much sense. In looking back, you may discover different qualities you have developed, understanding or other growth on subtle levels that you may have made.

You may also be working out a lot of karma or imbalance in your life. Look for the growth, the possibilities in these situations.

Pain and Suffering of the World

Many people find it difficult to handle the pain and suffering of others. Some persons become almost immobilized by it. When a person goes through this step and begins to feel the pain and suffering of the world—and not just one or a few persons—it can become overwhelming. When a person begins to open to this step it usually changes focus to one person. You will then experience what this person is experiencing. This step is not for the faint-hearted. During the experience, if you will truly go into it, you will be filled with a sense of peace and understanding. You will know why the other person is going through this, how they are learning and growing. You will sense a greater vision of negative events. You will recognize this may be the only way that they can learn a certain quality that they need to have. You will have comprehension

of the positive side of negativity. Also, you will understand how to turn those negatives into positives.

On pain and suffering, the best thing is to go into it.
It will hurt and you'll bawl and cry and all that stuff,
but it is the best way to go through it. Then you'll
come out with a real sense of peace.

After you have achieved this, you can work with
anybody on anything. It doesn't matter how bad the
event is, you will feel total compassion and empathy
for the person but you will not be attached to or
caught up in it. You can see what brought them to that
place and where they are going with it. You will get
the total picture of it and the universal sense of it.

Attachment–Job Syndrome

In this area you may lose all those things that you
over-valued or thought you needed. If you felt, for
instance, that education was very important, you may
find yourself in a situation where it is of no help. If
money has high priority, that may be lost. In more
extreme cases the family may turn against the person
and love relationships disappear. You may feel God
and the universe have abandoned you.

However, what comes from this level is a deeper
connection with your Creator. A great appreciation of
things replaces attachment.

If you find yourself going through this, it is best to
give self, possessions, ego, and all your attachments
totally to God. Let yourself feel barren and empty in
your deepest regions. Then you will find you have
opened yourself to much greater possibilities and, as
was the case with Job, you will receive even more.

Some people willingly go through this by simplifying their lives and totally surrendering to destiny.

Seeing into Hell-like Areas

There may be very negative places within people as well as on the negative side of the lower astral plane. This is sometimes referred to as hell.

Sometimes in a person's meditation or quiet time they will see faces of people they do not know. Sometimes it will be persons from other lives or persons who are now on the astral plane. That is, the person has died but for some reason their energy is around you. If these faces seem distorted, angry or otherwise unpleasant then you know that you are seeing these faces from a lower level. You may actually be seeing the persons.

You may be approached by incredibly negative spirits or very lost spirits and they want to be saved from hell or they want you to work with them. They want you to do something. It manifests in different ways too horrible even to describe but they may be asking for help to come out. Most of them don't really want out. They want attention or they want your energy, which they will subvert to their own uses. What you can do is pray for release of those who genuinely want out and are supposed to be out. It is best to pray and leave it to God. Sometimes a person's ego gets involved and thinks that we're supposed to save everybody.

There are people in physical bodies who are negative in a similar way. They'll want your attention. This person generally has a murky, slimy yellow-green color in the aura. Its opposite is the beautiful radiant yellow-green of the person who is really working on her own growth. Anyway, the negative person just wants attention but doesn't intend to do anything with it. People like this will go from one growth group to another; one healer to another; one counselor to another. They have no intention of growing, they just want the attention and they feed on that. It feeds their own negative space. You need to learn not to be caught in that whether they are in the body or not in the body.

If you wish, you may pray for the persons, tell them to go to God. You should then feel that your vibrations are higher. Do this by letting yourself feel lighter and freer and feeling the presence of God in you and around you. One of the problems here is a person may find their energy pulled down. The test here is to recognize it when you can, and it may help to not be snagged by it.

Appropriateness

It is important to be careful where you use your energies because, although there is an inexhaustible supply from the divine level, there is only so much that can go through you. You are only so strong a transmitter and you can burn yourself out.

Also, you need to be careful to use your energies where they seem to be effective. Sharing or working with persons who are negative and reject what you do (even if he or she requested it) can bring negativity back to you. The message here is to be appropriate.

Loneliness

You will experience a tearing loneliness in the chest area. It's as though you're being torn apart in the chest and even if you have somebody you really love, that person can't satisfy the loneliness. It is a loneliness to have a stronger attachment to your soul level, to your higher self and to your Creator. It's that cosmic connection that is the source of your loneliness. Fill the painful area with love and hold it there. Love is the great connector and that heals the loneliness.

Sometimes when you're in this loneliness you'll find yourself pushing yourself away from people and that you're pushing them away because you are obsessed with the loneliness. Doing this allows you to love and to receive love back from other people in a much freer manner.

Faith during Quantum Leaps

Every once in a while you will feel as though a huge, huge change is coming. There is a feeling of disconnectedness and sometimes an inability to function well. It's as though there is no foundation, no grounding and you are being pushed to make changes that in your more rational moments seem pretty far-fetched. It's also as if you are pushed to the edge of the cliff and shown a much higher cliff several miles away with a huge drop-off in between. You feel the faraway cliff calling to you. It is calling you to take a leap of faith— to get to the new way of being. There is no way to go down the cliff, across and up the other one. It is impossible and you don't have time anyway. The call becomes more urgent. The following is a meditation to help you feel faith in your system, enough to make the leap of faith.

—Meditation—
Opening the Body to Faith

Close your eyes. Imagine yourself walking to the edge of a steep cliff. Look at the higher cliff some miles away. Feel it pulling you forward. Then imagine that you jump over there, walk through the air or fly to this other cliff. As you are on the other cliff—be in open meditation and ask what are other possibilities.

Another version of this meditation is to imagine a new project or opportunity on the far cliff and when you arrive there feel it begin to manifest for you.

Doing this type of exercise helps to alert your body that the big changes are really okay.

Way Stations or Places to Grow

There will be way stations along the path, places that feel like home. This relates to teachings you will receive, teachers you may encounter, or a religion, whichever you feel is the right one. "I have found home, I have answers, it's going to be great now. I have my teacher, my guru and it's going to be great and it is for a while." This can sometimes be called "blind devotion" and that can be a trap into looking for the perfect answer, the perfect thing.

What you do is whatever your way station is at the moment. While you are there, learn from it—experience it. How can you grow from it but not be attached and with no blind devotion? Appreciate and learn.

Then your next way station may be higher than that or may be lower than that. You may choose after a particularly intense high period of working on spiritual growth to go work in gardens for a year or two. It may seem lower but it isn't really—it's just filling in places in the body. You also need to not be caught in whatever is higher or lower but open to what you need right now. That's the main thing and it gives you freedom on your path.

You are on this planet for a relatively fast evolutionary process in terms of the whole cosmic scheme. It may seem slow to us but it's relatively fast compared to some other things. If you were living on Mars or Saturn, the astrologers may say your Earth energy is strong. You are into evolving and growing. Mars has strength, Venus has love, and Earth has growth energy. So there is a reason you are on a planet that has this particular frequency of energy with it. You have chosen to speed your evolution by reincarnating on earth. Learn as much as you can from this way station.

Choice over Life and Death

Never before in our history have we had such control over life and death. New methods to aid in giving birth are available as are new methods in terminating life or prolonging it. Abortions, birth control, euthanasia are all parts of forcing us to see ourselves as co-creators with God in our approaches to life. Each person must face his or her own belief system and personal destiny in order to decide what is best.

Arms Outstretched

Sometimes in your meditation or quiet time you may feel yourself or see yourself on the side of a mountain or balcony or some other higher level with your arms outstretched and many people below. Many people see this, do not understand it, and do not share it lest they be thought presumptuous and putting themselves up. In actuality this will happen to people when they reach a certain level of development and it is a call to be Christ-like, to follow in the Master's footsteps, to let love flow through you, to be a channel of love to go to many people.

You may find that in addition to the love, you are also a channel of healing, knowledge, wisdom, or strength. If you have had this vision go back to it, try to be in the feelings of it again. What were the qualities that you were aware of? Did you feel healing flow through you, knowledge, wisdom, strength? Did you let the love flow through? Meditate on this and let yourself open up to whatever seemed the strongest.

Initiations

Various spiritual groups have their own initiations and they sometimes have very powerful effects on people. However, there are very powerful forces that bring initiations to you from the spiritual realms by reason of your growth and development. As you reach a certain stage in your growth the initiation happens automatically. It's as though your energy pattern attracts it. There are two types—one is the spiritual or heavenly initiation and the other is from the earth. They, too, have various energies within them and relate to various areas of growth. All of them open your consciousness to greater knowledge and abilities. When they happen a person needs to take extra time to ponder or think. Rather take the time to let the thoughts think themselves. It's as though new ideas were poured into your being and by paying attention to them they become part of your awareness. Subjects of the spiritual nature include para-religion (going beyond earthly patterns to universal laws); continuity of life, past, present, and future; relationships; superhuman abilities, and many more. The Earth initiations bring you closer to nature and give greater understanding of Earth and its purpose.

In earlier growth, people are usually not aware they are receiving initiations. Quite often, they happen when a person is sleeping, as the system is quieter and more receptive. In later stages of growth, people are more aware of what is happening.

Spiritual initiations come down through the top of the head and go through the body. They feel and look like lightning bolts. Sometimes they trigger Kundalini releases.

Earth initiations come from the feet up through the body. They, too, can trigger Kundalini release. A person may experience a lot of heat with Earth initiations.

Both types can leave a person rattled and with the feeling of being opened to a greater consciousness. The effect may continue for weeks or months and extra time alone is necessary. Just letting one's mind wander or writing is helpful. Another indication of having received an initiation is that your actions and reactions are so different.

Getting the Most from Your Tests and Steps

Each person goes through their own tests, their own steps. No one else can do it for them. Every time you have learned what you needed to, whether you understood it or not, you have made growth. Sometimes you will repeat certain things until you do understand what you are learning. In spiritual growth it is not enough to be able to merely accomplish something, but you must also develop an understanding of what is happening. Whether you feel a situation is a test or step, or just one of life's opportunities for growth and creativity, always look at it. What can you learn from it? How can you balance it? Then turn it to positive. Taking this attitude will speed your growth. There is no problem that does not have a solution. Finding solutions brings understanding and creativity and opportunities for action.

A very helpful attitude towards problems can be that of genuine appreciation and thanks to God for the problem, knowing that it brings growth. You can begin by praying and giving thanks for the particular problem. When you find that you genuinely mean it, then you know you have made a lot of growth.

When you feel that things are unbearable, it may be helpful to remember what St. Paul wrote in his first letter to the Corinthians, Chapter 10, Verse 13: "God keeps faith, and He will not allow you to be tested above your powers, but when the test comes He will at the same time provide a way out, by enabling you sustain it."

There are other tests and steps that people go through. However, those listed in this chapter should help you understand and identify the process.

Chapter XII

REINCARNATION COUNSELING

MORE PEOPLE ARE RECOGNIZING that some of their problems are genetic, traits inherited from ancestors. Now an ever-growing number of people are also recognizing that some of their problems stem from their own past lives.

A new field of therapy is developing as therapists are exploring and training in this area to help this increasing need.

Clearing out the past, being reassured of the future are all parts of understanding the bigger process in which we are involved. We need to trust this process more if for no other reason than it can explain what we are doing on this earth. This process of evolution is our main purpose on earth. By counseling from this concept, a person is given a bigger picture of oneself and

God's divine plan for her or him. It makes it easier to not get so caught up in things.

Counseling for Children

Many younger children have past life memories that sometimes need healing. Children usually do well in understanding reincarnation even from short explanations. It helps them face the deaths of friends, pets, and even their own. It can also help explain some bad dreams or memories.

Care should be used if you live in an area opposed to reincarnation. Not giving your child too much information may keep them from being ridiculed by others if they decide to educate the neighborhood children! Some children seem to know instinctively how much to share and how much is best kept to themselves or their families.

Adults

Adults find past life counseling helpful in a variety of ways. Relationships and the inability to make real progress in life seem to be two of the main issues. The main benefit in regressions, however, seems to be the sense that life really is eternal and that there is a greater plan for each person. A sense of that continuity can be very helpful.

Death

There are a number of ways to approach a person regarding his coming death. Usually letting him explain what he thinks and feels about his life, first, then secondly his death, can be helpful. Discussing the possible attitudes and feelings about death listed in the beginning of Chapter VIII may help expand their ability to get in touch with their own thoughts and feelings.

Chapter VIII has a number of ideas that can be adapted for counseling. The following questions may also help open the dialogue:

1. What accomplishments of yours have you especially appreciated this life?

2. How have you grown in qualities, especially love?

3. What have you wanted to be or do but haven't as yet? Are these desires draining you?

4. What can you do now in order to complete or release these desires?

5. What people do you wish to be with again in another life?

6. What people do you *not* wish to be with again in another life? There would be a need to release all feelings towards that person including the desire not to see them again. It's easier in the long run to work things out, at least for yourself.

7. How do you feel past lives enriched this one?

8. How will this life enrich future ones?

9. Do you need to forgive yourself, others, or situations so you don't drag the heaviness with you into the future?

10. Have you learned to be yourself with others?

11. Have you learned to *be*?

12. Are you continuing to develop your spiritual self so the transition of death is easier and life on the other side is stronger?

Future of Reincarnation Counseling

More people are seeking out information regarding their past lives, as well as experiencing this information through regressions. As a counseling tool, only the surface of this has been broken through. As more and more people see the current life as a part of the greater whole, the need for guidance and counseling in these areas will increase.

Chapter XIII
NATURE AND ANIMALS

HAVE YOU EVER HAD A PET that did the same tricks or acted the same way as another deceased pet? Chances are it has reincarnated to be with you again. Pets usually return as the same kind of animal. Love, trust, and supportiveness are basic reasons for being together again.

On occasion the returns can be considered karmic. We regressed a woman who at that time had over twenty cats in her home—all well cared for with regular vet trips. She was very good to them. In her past life she had severely mistreated cats, even torturing them. She couldn't relate to that life she had changed so much.

When animals die they spend time on the astral level and may hang around their owners for quite a while. We once moved into a house complete with a ghost dog. The previous owner's deceased pet was still hanging around. He didn't mind us or the kitten we later acquired. However, when the kitten died, that was too much. He didn't want the company on the astral plane.

When we have pets or plants with us and in our consciousness, we help them develop. Usually if there is a strong bond, the pet or plant won't resonate that much with its group soul. Instead, it comes under our influence.

The pets and plants in turn help us expand our awareness beyond our normal consciousness.

Reincarnating as Animals

Beliefs vary on whether humans ever become or return to the animal kingdom or below. In the thousands of regressions I have done I've never seen an instance of this. It doesn't mean it doesn't happen. It just means I haven't seen it! However, in taking people back to pre-human times, many have experienced the animal kingdom.

It is entirely possible that some people may choose to return to being an animal for a lifetime. It could be that being human doesn't seem as appealing. However, this could slow down general evolution.

If a person's development has been similar to the vibrations of plants, insects, or animals, they may prefer to stay on the level after death. They would have great ability to influence the plants, animals, or insects. It is entirely possible that a person may then choose to reincarnate on that level. We have an incredible amount of free will.

Land Areas

When a person has a powerful experience some of the energy remains at the particular location. If in later lives you go back to that spot, you will receive some more of the energy. If you are very intuitive you will probably remember some of what went on during that time.

When you have studied or had a strong spiritual experience in a temple or other religious area, some of that energy also remains there—which you can touch into through resonance and intent.

The following is a meditation that may bring some of that to today's consciousness.

—Meditation—
Accessing Past-Life Growth from Land Areas

Be in a meditative state. Ask to resonate with learning or an experience at a spiritual center during past lives at the following areas (one at a time). You may wish to imagine you are there once again:

- ✦ *Peru*
- ✦ *Mexico*
- ✦ *Tibet*
- ✦ *Japan*
- ✦ *Palestine*
- ✦ *Stonehenge*

You may wish to include some other place for which you feel a resonance or attraction.

*You may also wish to include wherever you
do your spiritual studying this life.*

*Write down the information and review it at a
later date. You may find you gather more information.*

Power Spots

Some areas of land have unusually strong vibrations
of particular kinds and are called *power spots*. When
people visit these power spots, usually they add to its
energy, thus creating an even more powerful spot. In
some cases, people actually drain enough power from
the area that it seems to lose its power and goes "out
of fashion."

Sometimes the energy of past happenings will leave
an imprint on the land, which affects people.

Cities and heavily populated areas will drain energy
from earth if there aren't enough trees and other vege-
tation to balance the human drain.

Chapter XIV
FUTURE

EVERY BREATH WE TAKE, shallow or deep, hesitant or free, helps determine our future. Every bit of love, joy, and other good qualities helps brighten and improve our future. Every bit of negativity or despair mishandled darkens and slows down future growth and achievements.

Also how we breathe, how we relate to things and people now are set in motion by our past or by energy of the future. Only in the present can we make changes. Past and future affect us, but it's in the present we let go, change or improve things. Action is in the now. Through this action we put our growth to practice, we move ourselves further along our evolutionary path or, perhaps, sidetrack it or slow it down depending on what it is we do!

Ripeness/Maturity

Many times a person will feel he has achieved his goals, that he has completed evolution. It may well be that the goals or purposes for this life or a particular part of this life have been completed. This happens for many people. This completeness (or what can be called a ripeness/maturity) is only the beginning for new levels of evolution. Even people nearing the end of their lives will find that new learning or new philosophies are still available.

All things have a ripeness or maturity in their development. This means the energy is at peak usability. When this happens a person feels able, confident, and on-target with whatever they do. However, unlike fruit or vegetables that rot after reaching their peak, when people reach their peak with something, it attracts new energy and new abilities. The process then starts over on a higher or deeper level. This will be even more evident as we are progressing in these seemingly accelerated times.

Ripeness/Maturity with the Body

The body of the future will stay youthful much longer and be more flexible. The ripeness/maturity will bring a new kind of beauty—soul beauty. Soul energy gives a more youthful, ageless look because the soul itself is from the eternal level and doesn't know death or aging.

Ripeness/Maturity with Astrological Energy

This will be a time at which a person will have figured out how to use the tools the astrological energy gives her or him. It will make accomplishment of anything

much easier because people will know the best ways
to use planetary energy.

Ripeness/Maturity of Soul Development

When a person's personality and ego are filled and
guided with soul energy, then the greatest development possible will be made in the earthly life.

Any negative thing a person does will not reach the
soul. It resides beyond the realm of negativity and only
feels the positive development. The soul invests in the
personality/ego as a way of developing itself further.
When negatives happen, empty places are not filled in
the soul and the soul may have to invest in more incarnations in order to achieve its goals of full consciousness and development. When the soul sends its energy
into a new being, the new being picks up the karma
that had gathered in earlier incarnations.

Ripeness/Maturity in Relationships

When people reach this level, the relationship opens to
a universal form—friends forever. You may not like or
approve of what the other person does, however, your
love is unconditional and non-judgmental.

Ripeness/Maturity with Nature

When you've made this connection, plants, animals,
and other aspects of nature are very open to you.
Communication back and forth is easy. Plants, animals, other nature beings, and earth can call to you
easily. Also you will open to a depth of connection you
never thought possible. Generally speaking, humans
have only scratched the surface of communicating and
relating with nature.

Ripeness/Maturity with Career

When you've reached this stage you need to start blending in other things or reach for new levels as the energy will have such a forward movement. Sometimes people will take on new careers when this stage has been reached in the current life.

Oneness is something most of us strive for and it is wonderful. However, we also need to reach the ripeness/maturity level; this also means action energy is present. A person is at the peak of functioning and ready for more.

Better Future

That is the story of our evolution. Learn something well, and new things to learn will automatically unfold. When we work with this process we are more consciously able to help choose the new energies and abilities.

Further suggestions for helping prepare for a better future are:

1. The Golden Rule: "Do unto others as you would have others do unto you" is great. However, you also need to be aware that the other person may not be practicing the Golden Rule. You may need to put energy back in yourself that helps prevent people from taking advantage of you. "Do" from your strength and not because you are hooked in.

2. The process of life is one of growing and learning. Always have something to study and be open to growing.

3. Unconditional love is sometimes very difficult. However, it can save you a lot of pain and heartache if you can achieve unconditional love, even part of the time.

4. Awareness—what's going on, why, where, and what you should do about it, if anything. Sometimes we are too quick to act.

5. Include service to others in your life. Little things that you do give you a deeper awareness of others and brightens people's lives. Do be careful that you don't keep them from learning through their experiences by being over-willing to help.

6. Don't leave loose ends in relationships if possible. If closure is not possible, then let loose. Don't hang on.

7. Developing your spiritual awareness includes learning about life after death. Fear of life after death can hold you back. Some people aren't afraid of death so much as they are of what may happen afterwards. Death means you let go of the body and anything connected to the body. Whatever the emotions and thoughts you die with, you carry over into your next life. If negative, they may hamper growth between lives. Some people find that planning possibilities for future lives helps give them a better perspective about death.

8. We need to develop the ability to change genetic patterns—for the better. Whatever you change affects the entire family. Also you may choose to come back in the same genetic stream and you'll appreciate what you've done before.

9. You can't always ask for forgiveness. There are things you just need to get straightened out. You can ask for help—your Creator is still working in and through you. Understanding what went wrong many times brings the forgiveness through a release. Forgiveness without understanding can leave you vulnerable to a similar experience until you learn the lesson.

10. Always face situations—these are opportunities from which you can grow.

11. Stop "packing the suitcase." Lose ego attachment. Quit packing karma to take with you for your next life.

12. You can learn to stop the karmic wheel of action between you and others by not acting negatively.

13. Don't push what won't go. Things have their due time. Prepare for the due time, then you can get the best from it.

14. Be aware of your needs and others' needs in a relationship.

15. Be truthful to the self. Be open to the energy or vibrations of what is going on at the moment. You can make better choices there.

16. Allow others their maintenance duties in relationships. They need an investment. If you do everything in a relationship, the other person doesn't feel needed.

17. Be fair to yourself and others.

18. Remember that evolution moves, and moves *through* us. Therefore, action is a necessary

part of life. We need to be aware of right
action and do it.

Living right helps you transcend into the higher spiritual level because the energy is lighter and freer.

Time Travel

Traveling back in time and into future time has long
interested many people. As we progress in consious-
ness, time travel will become even more important as
an aspect of our growth.

It is possible to go back in time with full consciousness or in hypnosis by going into the holographic universe and connecting with the akasha vibration, which
contains records of past and present lives and potential
future lives. Going into the future is more difficult
probably because the probable futures do not have as
strong an impact in the akashic records as events that
have actually happened.

Psychics or spiritually developed people have been
born with, and have developed, an ability to look into
the past or into the future as well as more deeply into
the present. On occasion people have experienced
spontaneous views into the past or the future, or they
may have seen something currently happening at
another location.

Memories can reactivate whole scenes so strong you
can see certain things that weren't available before.

Traveling physically to the past and future has long
been the dream of many. This would be very difficult
to do since the physical body is composed of dense

matter and bound more to the present than, say, the emotional, mental, or spiritual aspects of the self.

There have been reports of a number of people who have achieved bi-location. The soul creates a duplicate body to appear someplace other than where the first body is located. Love and concern for another seems to be a motivating factor.

If the soul can create a second body to appear in different spaces, certainly it is conceivable that it could create a body to appear in different time periods and, perhaps, even interact with a person's previous body.

One thing that does seem to occur, although rarely, is that a scene from the past will spontaneously appear in physical form. On rare occasions, people interact with those in the scene. Usually they just watch and sometimes people in the past life scene are aware of them. It's as though some like-vibration resonates with the past scene and causes it to reappear.

As people develop more, and their consciousness raises higher, more of these events should happen.

Calling Forth Past Scenes

It is possible sometimes to call forth a scene from the past that happened in the area where you are. The following is a meditation exercise you may wish to try.

—Meditation—
Calling Forth Past Scenes

Be outdoors in an open area. You may sit or stand. With gentle breathing, feel yourself connecting with the earth. When you feel in connection, ask to see a scene that has happened in that area sometime before. Sit quietly, loosely, and don't focus your eyes too much. Let the scene appear.

One workshop person reported seeing a scene where an Indian man and boy were walking along. The boy stepped into his form, stopped for a moment as if he realized something was different, and then continued his journey. When the apparition of the boy was in his body, he became aware that they were part of a group that was going to join a larger group. He was aware of other thoughts and feelings as well.

Sometimes in the scene the people appear as apparitions not having a dense physical body. Other times the bodies appear as real as ours.

Sometimes an area will change in such a strong manner that you can actually touch the material things or people from the scene.

At the rate technology is advancing, we're sure there will someday be a machine facilitating experiences of the past and the future. It may also show different probable paths a person could have taken or might yet take.

For the present, regressions into past lives and progressions into future lives are the best way to experience these other timeframes.

The Future Is Temporarily Planned

Our future in this life and others is temporarily planned, based on forces we have either set in motion or previously blocked. We are coming into a period of greater intuitional, mental, and spiritual development, which will help us be more aware of what is or is not manifesting in our lives and what we can do about it.

The more aware we are of the future, the more we can, with our understanding, intent, and actions, reprogram this life and future lives.

In order to do this well, we need the courage to look at seemingly negative things that may make our lives better. Also, we may see that we have to give up some desires and enhance others in order to achieve better, happier, and more productive lives. The fear of what will be seen and that it may not be grand enough can hold back a willingness to open to what's in motion. One needs faith in oneself and in one's Creator, as well as faith in the overall goodness of evolution in order to really look at one's patterns and directions.

Dreams, intuitions, and insights all let us know some of what's transpiring. People trained to look into the future can also be helpful. The main thing is for a person to open to overall development that can bring greater awareness, so better choices can be made. Another helpful reminder is that this is just one of many lives. We don't have to make all of our growth at once. However, the most important life is always the current one. That is the one with which you may have the most effect.

Bibliography

Hawking, Stephen. *A Brief History of Time*. New York: Bantam Books, 1988.

Head, Joseph and S. L. Cranston. *Reincarnation: An East-West Anthology*. Wheaton, IL: The Theosophical Publishing House, 1961.

———. *Reincarnation*. New York: Causeway Books, 1967.

Paulson, Genevieve Lewis. *Kundalini and the Chakras*. St. Paul, MN: Llewellyn Publications, 1991.

Powell, Arthur E. *The Causal Body*. Wheaton, IL: The Theosophical Press.

Sandmel, Samuel (General Editor). *The New English Bible*. New York: Oxford University Press, Inc., 1976.

Talbot, Michael. *The Holographic Universe*. USA: Harper-Perennial, 1991.

Index

A

after life, 107-124

akasha, *also* askashic records, 18, 77-81, 83-87, 94, 99, 181

animals, 22, 25-26, 28-29, 171-173, 177

astrological energy, 65, 176

attachment, 16, 41, 43, 80, 153, 156-157, 160, 180

B

Big Bang, 23

birth(s), 128, 144, 162

multiple, 129

Black Holes, 56

bleedover, 55, 79, 90

blessings, 48-49, 68, 85, 97, 132

H

I

J

K

☾ REACH FOR THE MOON

Llewellyn publishes hundreds of books on your favorite subjects! To get these exciting books, including the ones on the following pages, check your local bookstore or order them directly from Llewellyn.

ORDER BY PHONE

- Call toll-free within the U.S. and Canada, 1-800-THE MOON
- In Minnesota, call (651) 291-1970
- We accept VISA, MasterCard, and American Express

ORDER BY MAIL

- Send the full price of your order (MN residents add 7% sales tax) in U.S. funds, plus postage & handling to:

    Llewellyn Worldwide
    P.O. Box 64383, Dept. K511-8
    St. Paul, MN 55164–0383, U.S.A.

POSTAGE & HANDLING

(For the U.S., Canada, and Mexico)

- $4.00 for orders $15.00 and under
- $5.00 for orders over $15.00
- No charge for orders over $100.00

We ship UPS in the continental United States. We ship standard mail to P.O. boxes. Orders shipped to Alaska, Hawaii, The Virgin Islands, and Puerto Rico are sent first-class mail. Orders shipped to Canada and Mexico are sent surface mail.

International orders: Airmail—add freight equal to price of each book to the total price of order, plus $5.00 for each non-book item (audio tapes, etc.).

Surface mail—Add $1.00 per item.

Allow 2 weeks for delivery on all orders.
Postage and handling rates subject to change.

DISCOUNTS

We offer a 20% discount to group leaders or agents. You must order a minimum of 5 copies of the same book to get our special quantity price.

FREE CATALOG

Get a free copy of our color catalog, *New Worlds of Mind and Spirit.* Subscribe for just $10.00 in the United States and Canada ($30.00 overseas, airmail). Many bookstores carry *New Worlds*—ask for it!

Visit our web site at www.llewellyn.com for more information.

Soul Healing

Dr. Bruce Goldberg

George: overcame lung cancer and a life of smoking through hypnotic programming.

Mary: tripled her immune system's response to AIDS with the help of age progression.

Now you, too, can learn to raise the vibrational rate of your soul (or subconscious mind) to stimulate your body's own natural healing processes. Explore several natural approaches to healing that include past life regression and future life progression, hypnotherapy, soulmates, angelic healing, near-death experiences, shamanic healing, acupuncture, meditation, yoga, and the new physics.

The miracle of healing comes from within. After reading *Soul Healing*, you will never view your life and the universe in the same way again.

1-56718-317-4 $14.95
304 pp., 6 x 9

The Search for Grace

The True Story of Murder and Reincarnation

Dr. Bruce Goldberg

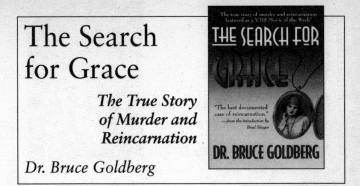

An unsolved murder mystery on the books since 1927 ... one modern woman's obsession with an abusive lover ... and a karmic journey that winds through a maze of past lives—all of these unite into the *best*-documented case of reincarnation in the Western world.

The Search for Grace is the true story of Ivy, a 26-year-old pharmacist who sought the help of Dr. Bruce Goldberg to put a stop to her inexplainable attraction to John, her physically and psychologically abusive boyfriend. Under hypnosis, she discovered that John had been her lover—and her murderer—in 20 of her 46 past lives.

When Ivy recounts the details of her 46th life as roaring-twenties party girl Grace Doze, hypnotherapy and real-life dovetail into a dramatic twist of fate. It was May 19, 1927, when the body of Grace Doze turned up in a Buffalo, N.Y., creek. Her murder remained a mystery until 60 years later, when Dr. Goldberg put Ivy into a superconscious state, and Grace's true killer was brought to light for the world to see.

What Happens After Death

Scientific & Personal Evidence for Survival

Migene González-Wippler

What does science tell us about life after death? How do the different religions explain the mystery? What is the answer given by the strange mystical science known as Spiritism? These and other questions about the life beyond are explored in *What Happens After Death*.

The first part of the book is an objective study of the research about life after death. The second part is a personal narrative by a spirit guide named Kirkudian about his various incarnations. While the two sections could be considered two separate books, they simply express the same concepts in uniquely different ways.

Experience for yourself one soul's journey through the afterlife, and discover the ultimate truth: that every soul is created in union with all other souls, and that we are all manifestations of one purpose.

1-56718-327-1   **$7.95**
5 3/16 x 8, 256 pp., softcover

After Death Communication

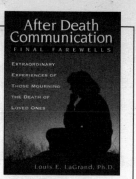

Final Farewells

Louis E. LaGrand, Ph.D.

"I saw my dead son standing in the hallway near the stairs to his bedroom. He was wearing a favorite hat. I wanted to believe he was happy." In this moving and compassionate work, a pioneer in after-death communication research guides you through one of the most empowering of human experiences.

Forty-two percent of people surveyed claim to have had some type of after-death contact with a loved one. This book examines a wide variety of those experiences—seeing, hearing, or sensing the presence of the deceased; feeling a touch; smelling a fragrance; meeting the loved one in a vision or dream; unusual appearances of birds and animals; and a host of other unexplainable happenings—all of which have provided millions of grieving people with relief that their loved ones still live on. Dr. LaGrand takes the experience out of the realm of illusion, and also shows how support persons can assist the bereaved to use these experience to go on with their lives.

1-56718-405-7 $12.95
6 x 9, 256 pp., softcover